Virtue
— from —
Adversity

THE MISSION HALLS OF GLASGOW

Virtue from Adversity
ISBN : 978-0-9561031-1-6

Published by

Christian Faith Ministries
Fraserburgh, Scotland
www.cfmscotland.com

Graphic Design by Darran Drysdale

Printed in Scotland by Bell and Bain Ltd, Glasgow.

Contents

Dedication

I dedicate this book to my wife

JEAN

with deepest gratitude to God for the 50+ years of ministry
we have enjoyed together in song, word and music.
Also for the support received and encouragement given
during the many days of trial and testing which God
providentially allowed to come into our lives in order that
Christian character could be developed for HIS glory.

Foreword

When Peter Drysdale told me of his intention to write a book about the Glasgow Mission Halls, I was initially quite excited at the prospect. But I confess that I then began to have some misgivings as to whether the book would arrive on the scene too late, because so many who had lived through that era, and who would have treasured the memories stirred by reading about it, had already gone from this life. Today we have a whole generation with no first-hand knowledge whatsoever of the significant impact which these centres of evangelism and amelioration made upon the lives of untold numbers of men, women and children in the city of Glasgow, and far beyond.

However, having read the book, I now find that my fears were unfounded, for in writing it, Peter has done his research very thoroughly, and has given to us an insight to the appalling social conditions in which many people lived – or perhaps we should say – existed, in those days. It was against this background that the conscience of good men began to be stirred, endeavouring to alleviate the lot of those who were unable to extricate themselves from the squalor and abject poverty of the times. It was during these days too, that Moody and Sankey came to Scotland, and to Glasgow in particular, resulting in the beginning of a great spiritual awakening from which emerged the divine stimulus for the work of the Mission Halls which were undoubtedly befitted "for such a time as this."

The book tells us not only about these centres of outreach, but explains some of the specific conditions which led to their commencement. I had come into touch from time to time with the work of the "Foundry Boys", but had no idea whatsoever of the dreadful conditions in which boys then worked, and which gave rise to the noble initiative of those who rose to the challenge to try to lift them from the mire of ignorance and poverty in which they lived and toiled.

Similarly, I knew of the work of the Canal Boatmen's Institute; but this book gives us a graphic insight to the sheer commercial importance of the Forth and Clyde, and other canals in the matter of transportation, long before the age of the Railways and Motorways of our times, and reminds us that those who were employed in this sector had deep social and spiritual needs, in response to which the Institute was founded.

I personally owe a great deal to my early days in the Glasgow Mission Halls, particularly Bethany Hall and Tent Hall, where the challenge of the Christian Gospel first impacted my life. The Saturday night tea meetings; the testimonies of transformed lives; the fervency of the prayer meetings; the warm-heartedness of the people, have left an indelible impression upon my mind. I had a "deputation party" and usually a full diary of Saturday night tea meeting engagements from October to March each year, where with those who so faithfully supported me week by week, we visited many of these small corner shop missions, and had the opportunity to gain experience in communicating the message of salvation through singing, testimony and preaching.

To those who lived through that era, this book will stimulate the memory of those times. The excellent proliferation of photographs greatly enhances the narrative. And to a younger generation who knew nothing of the spiritual atmosphere of the Tent Hall packed to capacity with more than two thousand people listening intently to the Gospel being preached in great power; or of the more intimate environment of a small mission hall, with the smell of the tea being brewed - or perhaps it was stewed - and the equally effective communication of the message by the testimony and preaching of a group of young enthusiasts, I am sure that "Virtue from Adversity" will be a worthwhile and informative record of a significant epoch in the history of Glasgow.

I heartily commend the book to a wide readership.

Gordon Haxton

Chapter One

THOSE WERE THE DAYS

Simone Signoret, the French actress once said that, "nostalgia is not what it used to be." However, if you enter the word *nostalgia* into Google, the search engine will report over thirty million hits and this would tend to negate Miss Signoret's statement. Speaking personally, and conceding that it is probably a function of advancing years, I take the opposite point of view. What can be more pleasant on a winter's evening than sitting in a nice warm room with subdued lighting while reflecting on days gone by plus the family, friends and places associated with them?

The Oxford Dictionary defines nostalgia as *sentimental longing or wistful affection for the past* and, if it is ever declared to be a crime, I will immediately plead guilty. The book that you are currently holding in your hand is a product of a chronic case of nostalgia and I offer no apology for it!

As we review the tapestry that our life has woven, every one of us can recall conflicting times of sadness and happiness. I am no different and one of my times of very happy memories, or more correctly, a series of very happy memories, occurred when I was in my teens and a-courting a young lady who eventually became my wife; a post she has now held for almost half a century. She had – and still has – a beautiful soprano voice and, at that time, sang in a quintet with four other girls from an Evangelical Fellowship in Kilsyth – a town in Scotland's Central Belt, 12 miles east of Glasgow and half way along the road to Stirling. The Fellowship in question was known as *The Westport Hall* and, back then, it was one of the brightest lights in Scotland as far as Spirit-filled ministry and singing was concerned. The President of the work at that time was a man called Harry Tee. As well as being a highly respected man of God in the community, Mr Tee was a prolific song writer whose lyrics were replete with both fundamental and deeper points of sound Biblical doctrine. His songs live on today.

As the quintet became more accomplished in their singing ministry, their diaries became more populated with invitations from near and far. The *near* included the city of Glasgow and many a Saturday saw the famous five, their accompanist (May McFarlane) and their fan club boarding a bus in Kilsyth for a meeting or social event in the metropolis. At that time, Glasgow still had her famous tramcars (natively and affectionately known as *caurs*).

Having disembarked at Dundas Street bus terminus, the singing band would board one of these vehicles and be transported, with the sound of *clanging*, through the streets of the city to their destination. Many times that destination would prove to be one of Glasgow's legendary Mission Halls. I became fascinated, and fell in love, with these places. They all had their own individual ethos and atmosphere and they all had unique characters and one-of-their-kind *worthies* included in their regular congregations. My series of very happy memories is, therefore, having had the privilege of living during the time when some of the Mission Halls had maybe passed their zeniths and yet it was still an honour to attend and witness the activities which took place in their famous venues.

Two decades later, after a five year employment stint in London, I returned to work one mile west of Glasgow city centre and, for the next number of years, experienced the legendary warmth of the populace. Glasgow is a fantastic city. The pavement humour is natural and spontaneous; it was there half a century ago in the Mission Hall days; I witnessed it over a quarter of a century later in my work-a-day life in the city and it is still there today as I type these words. I only wish I had launched this project some years ago because many of the characters I mentioned above have now gone to be with their Lord and cannot therefore be included in my research. Like all missed opportunities, we cannot press a *life-rewind* button, and this one must therefore join the ranks of my many "if only ..." situations. That's the bad news. The good news is that there are still people around who can recall those nostalgic days and my quest has been to find as many of them as possible and incorporate their input along with my archival research.

The old music hall song ended with the words *Glasgow belongs to me* and when first or second time strangers visit the city they can share that feeling with the local population. It's just the nature of the place; it's just how Glasgow is; it's just Glasgow! The natives *are* friendly whether they are shop assistants, white collar businessmen, blue collar transport staff or the city constabulary – colloquially known as the *polis*.

Today, Glasgow is a noticeably exciting and vibrant city. Over the past number of years the architecture has taken every opportunity to dress itself in ultra-modern fashion; the transport infrastructure has improved exponentially and the retail shopping facilities have promoted the city into the Premier League. But it wasn't always like that.

The Glasgow of yesteryear had more than her fair share of visible economic depression and obvious social deprivation. The traditional shipbuilding and steel industries were getting past their sell-by dates and the resulting redundancies and lay-offs had knock-on effects in poor housing stock and violent crime statistics. Globally, and in some ways unfairly, the city gained a bad reputation and, even today, is still having to live it down with some people who have too long memories or blunt axes to grind.

It is a paradox, but bad *can* beget good. In the 16th century, Lord Francis Bacon wrote that, "*Prosperity doth best discover vice, but adversity doth best discover virtue.*" This was certainly the case in Glasgow's *adversity* because one of the *virtues* that resulted from the early 20th century depression was that many of the Mission Halls that had appeared in the thoroughfares of the city earlier in the century, or at the close of the previous century, were filling up with people who needed a source of comfort in their hour of need. These spiritual oases were providentially available in all main points of the city's compass – north, south, east and west – and provided a much-needed resource at a critical time in the history of Glasgow.

It is so natural, logical, and reasonable to think that the everyday events of life are simply *happenstances*. However, the prophet Daniel had the task of informing a despotic king named Nebuchadnezzar that *"the Most High rules the kingdom of men"* and, from the inspired pen of the Apostle to the Gentiles, we learn that, behind the often inexplicable and perplexing vistas of life, there is an unseen hand belonging to the One *"who works all things according to the counsel of His will."* In retrospect, we can see this principle was operating in the spiritual life of Glasgow.

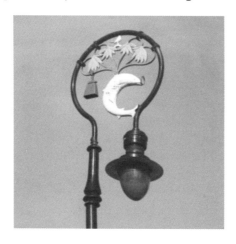

The picture above was taken in Cathedral Square and it displays, on an ornate lamp post, the city's coat of arms which has been in existence since 1866. It contains four symbols – a bird, a tree, a bell and a fish, and they all have an association with St Mungo. This patron saint, and the city of Glasgow, date back a long way because he was responsible for building a monastery on the banks of one of the tributaries of the River Clyde as early as the 6th century.

He is also credited with the words of the city motto, *Let Glasgow Flourish.* These three words are a truncation of a prayer he used during a sermon when he said, *"Lord, let Glasgow flourish by the Preaching of your Word and the Praising of Your Name."* His prayer was certainly answered because Glasgow *was* flourishing by the preaching of His

Word. God was at work in the Mission Halls and, through His Holy Spirit, lives were being changed. Personal testimonies of Divine grace and mercy were aplenty from those who had previously been held captive by Satan and who were now enjoying the freedom that can only be experienced by those whom the Son has set free.

This volume is not meant to be a formal treatise or dissertation on Glasgow's Mission Halls but rather a brief overview of their birth, their life and sadly, in many cases, their demise. I trust it will provide some nostalgia for the more mature citizens who can still recall these days; I expect it will probably provide some previously unknown historical information for those in the younger age brackets and, above all, I pray that it will be an encouragement and a springboard to action for all who are seeking today to obey Jesus Christ's final "*Go ye ...*" commission.

Let's not forget that it was HE who, while on planet earth for His first visit, gave an unconditional guarantee, "*I will build MY Church*" and, as the following chapters will show, it certainly included the Mission Halls of Glasgow.

Chapter Two

THE G.U.E.A.

GLASGOW IN THE 1870s

Before turning to the main subject of our current chapter, let us briefly consider the social and religious conditions which were prevalent in Glasgow in the 1870s.

One of the city of Glasgow's finest and greatest cultural resources is, unquestionably, the world-famous Mitchell Library in North Street and, while researching there, I obtained a copy of two interesting reports; the first one is titled *Lessons for the Time* (dated February 1879); the other one is titled *Report on the Religious Conditions of Glasgow* (dated January 1871). While studying these documents, the philosophical musings of King Solomon sprang to mind when he declared, "*there is nothing new under the sun.*" Why do I say that? Because the conditions described in both reports could easily have been written in more recent times to depict the Glasgow – and Scotland – of today.

The *Lessons for the Time* booklet is sub-titled *An Address in* Connection *with the Late Financial Disasters in Glasgow* and this presentation was given by the Rev. A. N. Somerville D.D. at the anniversary meeting of the United Evangelistic Association.

Let me quote from his opening remarks :

> When, in May 1877, I left this country for the distant colonies, our city was, apparently, in the height of prosperity. Commercial speculation, the excitements of competition, stocks, sales of property, high prices, high rents, high wages, style, costliness of living, expensiveness of entertainments, luxury, profuse provision for amusement – in short, all that could betoken social distinction were in full display. But when I came back in October last, I found that a sudden collapse had taken place, that Glasgow was in sadness; that instead of being looked up to, as the type of prosperity, our city, from her unlooked-for disasters, from the stroke on her merchants, bankers and capitalists, the blow that had fallen on her trustees, defenceless women and orphans, her depression in trade, the dejection, poverty and multitude of her unemployed was an object of commiseration to the kingdom.
>
> God Himself has spoken in these calamities. He has administered rebuke. He has brought His moral government and overruling providence to remembrance and has summoned us to consideration and repentance. Alas for us, if the voice should be unheeded

When we consider the historical events of relatively recent vintage, with regard to banking and commerce scandals, the situation exactly mirrors the economic scenario described by Mr Somerville back in the 1870s. Towards the end of his talk, he challenged the Church by saying :

> The violent interruption our prosperity has received may serve as an occasion for improving the character of society in general, and of calling forth from the Christian part of it a brighter witness for the Truth.

Bridgegate c.1904

While this first document addressed Glasgow's economic issues, the subject of the second document can be deduced from its front page where we are informed that the Report was issued by the *Association for Promoting the Religious and Social Improvement of the City*. The fourteen page document makes depressing reading as it goes into detail about housing conditions, lack of education, and alcohol abuse, all of which were problems at that time. One positive aspect was the church attendance statistics and many ecclesiastical leaders would be drooling if they saw them equalled in their fellowships today.

However, the main part of the Report was a review of the activities of the city churches – both denominational and non-denominational – and their fragmented approach to reaching the lost.

In the *General Conclusions* section, at the end of the Booklet, the authors present the following statement :

> Thoughtful and earnest men are at last awaking to the conviction that unfortunate sectarian estrangements should not stand in the way of common Christian effort; that even though the workers in Christ's cause may be ranged under different banners, they may go forward together for the results desired by all; in short, that although there may not be incorporation there may be co-operation of the different sections of the Christian Church. And in work among the lapsed and ignorant masses may be found one of those common grounds of action which are welcome to all unprejudiced minds. What care the denizens of the degraded quarters of our city for the Shibboleths of mere party spirit? To every denomination – apart from its peculiar views of church government – is addressed the call to go down with its neighbour into the mire land of ignorance and vice, and rescue brothers and sisters perishing therein for lack of knowledge. It is indeed time that sectarian estrangements were, at least in such a clamant duty, laid aside. It behoves Christian churches and individuals to be more zealous and less jealous.

From these 130+ year old documents, we can envisage a City where education was found wanting, housing conditions were insanitary, alcohol was achieving its objective of bringing misery and poverty into families, commerce was in recession with resultant unemployment levels and, to crown it all, the Church was not living up to its Mission Statement.

At this challenging period in Glasgow's history, a male Evangelistic duo providentially appeared in Scotland from the United States of America.

MOODY AND SANKEY

Having sent the Pilgrim Fathers to the New World in 1620, two of the *Pilgrim Sons* returned to the shores of Britain in 1873. Their names were Dwight Lyman Moody and Ira David Sankey.

D.L. Moody   Ira D. Sankey

There was no radio, television or internet to announce their arrival and yet God visibly blessed their early efforts in Newcastle and Edinburgh. Thousands of people, from every stratum of society, sought and found the Lord.

Somehow, the good news of their exploits in the East reached the Capital of the West and in December 1873, with only four days of notice, over 100 clergymen and lay representatives of various Evangelical denominations came together to consider the possibility of inviting the itinerant evangelists to Glasgow. As a result of this gathering, the *United Evangelistic Committee* was formed.

The meeting delegates unanimously resolved that, firstly, an invitation would be extended to the Americans and that, secondly, a Noon Day Prayer Meeting would be instituted from 5 – 9 February 1874. Later on, Mr Moody referred to these gatherings as the *backbone* of his ministry.

THE CENTRAL CHOIR

John R. Miller was a Glasgow businessman in the firm of Forsyth, Miller & Co., an Ironfounders based in Mile End. He had attended some meetings in Edinburgh where Mr Moody had preached and Mr Sankey had led the congregational singing and had also sung some powerful solos. He felt that this dual responsibility gave Ira D. Sankey a very exhausting workload. On returning to Glasgow, he called together some of his friends whom he knew were not only consecrated Christians but had good voices and knowledge of music. They met together every Saturday afternoon to practise from *Sacred Songs and Solos*, Mr Sankey's songbook.

Ira D. Sankey arrived in Glasgow as Mr Miller's guest on the afternoon of Saturday 7 February 1874 while the choir members were rehearsing for a social to be held in Finnieston Free Church. The evangelist was so impressed with what he heard that he invited them to the platform of the City Hall the following morning to help him lead the praise at the opening meeting of the Glasgow Campaign.

Mr Moody repeatedly acknowledged the great value of the work done by this choir.

The Central Choir continued in existence for a long number of years under the leadership of Mrs W.M. Oatts and ministered not only within the city boundary but in places further afield.

THE 1874 MISSION

Sunday 8 February 1874 saw the commencement of a series of missions in various venues and areas of the city which eventually led to a Tent being erected on Glasgow Green in May and remaining on the Green till the month of September.

Glasgow Green was an area where many of the city's social outcasts slept rough at night; men and women whom Satan had already *stolen* and was now doing his best to *kill and destroy*.

Some of these people had previously held high positions in society but, through the curse and control of alcohol, were now reduced to living like animals but who were nevertheless people for whom Christ had died.

I don't know if the sight of these vagrants touched a chord in the souls of the workers but it is recorded that as many as 1,200 people would gather in the Tent on Saturday evenings not only to pray for the residents of, in modern parlance, *cardboard city* but also to ask God to use the Sunday Evangelistic services as a means of transforming the lives of the people in the East End of the city.

The Mission provided a stimulus to the spiritual life of the city and many churches found their membership rolls increasing both by new members being added through salvation and by no-longer-committed members returning to the fold through the moving of God's Holy Spirit.

A SPECIAL MEETING

A *special* meeting took place on the evening of 24 February 1874 in Ewing Place Congregational Church in West Campbell Street

The target audience was young men. The presence and power of God was evident and tangible and, when Mr Moody gave an appeal, 101 young men rose up and, by doing so, publicly proclaimed their desire to enlist in the service of Jesus Christ.

As I have researched and read the old records, I have discovered one adjective peppered through them – *ameliorative.* This word does not appear to be so commonly used in our language today but it was obviously an *in-word* back then. Its verb simply means to *improve* or *make better* and one of the outcomes of the 1874 Glasgow Mission was that, throughout the Christian community, a new sense of spiritual responsibility evolved and a much deeper compassion, in relation to the temporal needs of the City's poor and its social outcasts, became evident.

THE G.U.E.A. IS BORN

The United Evangelistic Committee had previously been formed in order to co-ordinate the Moody, Sankey Mission and it is reckoned that the *special* meeting held in Ewing Place contributed more than any other feature of the Crusade to the formal constitution of the Glasgow United Evangelistic Association (G.U.E.A.) two years later in 1876.

The original Board of Directors consisted of 41 men presided over by Alexander Allan, a Ship Owner based in 70 Great Clyde Street. Of the other members, 22 had *Rev.* pre-fixing their names; the remainder were City businessmen including iron founders, tea merchants and a boot maker. As a point of interest, the boot maker was a certain William Quarrier who would later come to fame as *The Orphan Homes of Scotland*, bearing his name, came into being in Bridge of Weir, Renfrewshire.

With the help of a member of the Mitchell Library staff, I obtained a copy of the 8 page Report detailing the first year's work of the G.U.E.A. The impression I got while reading the document was that many Christians in Glasgow during the period following the fruitful Moody and Sankey Crusade were extremely busy in the Lord's work and were actively committed in taking the Gospel to every tier of society in the city.

I have listed below the titles of the section headings in the Report and, from the adjectives and nouns used, we can imagine the scope of the campaign of Evangelistic effort and the targets at which the G.U.E.A. were aiming :

Noon Prayer Meeting
Ewing Place Young Men's Meeting
Young Converts or Fellowship Meeting
Deputations of Young Men
Model Lodging Houses
Tent on Glasgow Green
Sabbath Morning Breakfasts
170,000 Rations
Work among Neglected Children
Industrial Day School
Home for Neglected Children
Saturday Night Rescuing Band
Temperance Prayer Meeting
British Workman Public Houses
Brickfields at Midnight
Employment Bureau

The Report concludes with the following paragraph :

Our best thanks are due to the friends in town and country who, by donations of money, goods or clothing, have enabled us to carry sunshine to so many sin-blighted hearts. Also to those who daily remembered us at the throne of grace, and to the Glasgow press as a whole, but especially to the *North British Daily Mail* for frequent friendly notices of our work. We have purposely refrained from estimating spiritual results. In all our Meetings we have great cause to thank God for manifested power. The Theatre Meetings continue to be very largely owned in the conversion of sinners and the reviving of believers. We expected ere this either to have been formally organized as a distinct Young Men's Association, or united with the other Young Men's Societies in Glasgow. Glasgow needs *one* strong united vigorous Association of young men to do battle for the cause of truth, and rescue souls from going down to the pit. We are leaving no stone

> unturned in order to secure Union and trust it may yet be attained. We have waited long, but it is worth waiting for. Once it is clear that it cannot be, we shall lose no time in banding ourselves together. For the blessing vouchsafed during the past year, we give thanks to Almighty God. Let gratitude be seen in increased willingness to serve. When the Master has work, however arduous, may He find us ready to do His will and follow Him fully. Our day for labour is short; He cometh quickly; let us therefore, with the eye fixed on a living Christ, press forward, heart to heart in communion, and shoulder to shoulder in work.

THE CHRISTIAN INSTITUTE

Another report discovered in the Mitchell Library was from the North British Daily Mail, dated Saturday, October 11, 1879. The heading was *Christian Institute* and the sub-heading was *Opening by Lord Shaftesbury*. Here are short extracts from the article :

> The Glasgow Christian Institute, situated in Bothwell Street, was formally opened yesterday by the Earl of Shaftesbury. The ceremony took place in the large hall which was crowded with ladies and gentlemen. ... The proceedings were opened by the singing of the One Hundredth Psalm. The Rev. Dr Bonar then read a portion of the Scriptures and the Rev. Dr Marshall Lang engaged in prayer.

There then followed a speech by Mr J. Campbell White :

> My Lord Shaftesbury, my Lord Provost, ladies and gentlemen – There is a beautiful verse in the 107th Psalm where, speaking of God's dealings with men in stormy waters, we read,

17

> "*So he bringeth them unto their desired haven.*"
> In meeting here for the first time today, and attaining what has so long been in view, our first desire is to give thanks to God, by whose good hand upon us we have been brought to our desired haven. It is no wonder, therefore, that the family of workers, nearly 14,000 strong who form the societies now represented on this platform, who have been for long years without any home of their own, should have awakened sympathy in many hearts. It was this feeling which led to the meeting six years ago, at which the scheme was launched that today is happily accomplished, and the Christian Institute Committee was formed which now welcomes you here.

On the same visit to the Mitchell Library when I found the above newspaper report, I also came across the original minutes of the meeting which Mr White referred to in his speech; they started as follows :

> Among the numerous associations in Glasgow who have in view the promotion of religion among the young men of the city, and instruction of children, a want has long been felt – that of suitable accommodation which they could call their own. Their good work has consequently been somewhat hindered, and were the want supplied it is believed that the efficiency and success of the various institutions would be much advanced.

The date of that meeting was Tuesday 9 September 1873 and Mr J. Campbell White, a chemical manufacturer based in Rutherglen, and a G.U.E.A. vice-president, was elected chairman of the Committee.

The graphic below is a part of the 1873 Meeting Minutes. No computers or word processors back then, in fact the typewriter was still in its first decade of development, but there were people who were skilled at handwriting and, while the writer's style is maybe not quite *copperplate*, it is certainly readable.

Looking through the above minutes, it was interesting to note that, among those present, were representatives of four organisations, some of whom feature later in this book:

The Glasgow Young Men's Christian Association
The Glasgow Young Men's Society for Religious Improvement
The Glasgow Sabbath School Union
The Glasgow Foundry Boys Religious Society

Another interesting observation from the 1873 minutes is that, when listing those who were present at the meeting, the person taking the minutes used the word *sederunt* which one dictionary defines as a *prolonged sitting (as for discussion)*. How times and terms change!

The Bothwell Street Resource

The above photograph shows a 1911 view of the ornate building which, with its front on 64–100 Bothwell Street, filled an entire city centre block with Blythswood Street as its western boundary and West Campbell Street as its eastern boundary.

Years later, structures were added to both ends of the original building, the west wing became a Y.M.C.A. club; the east wing became the world-famous Bible Training Institute (B.T.I.) and the G.U.E.A. central offices. The mixture of building styles was apparently not very pleasing to some of the architectural purists but, from a spiritual viewpoint, some of the people who were graduates of the B.T.I. went out into the wider world and helped to build a greater and longer lasting edifice – the Church of Jesus Christ.

The B.T.I.

In the 1942 publication of the Jubilee of the B.T.I., one of the contributors wrote :

> In recording the memorable origin of the Institute, three impressions abide with us who record them fifty years afterwards.
>
> First, the Institute was born in a revival atmosphere when the grace of God was manifest upon leaders and led alike. Prayer for guidance abounded and the will to further the Kingdom of God at home and abroad was greatly stimulated. To preserve and perpetuate this same blessing is the aim of all connected with the Institute.
>
> Second, from the very start the Institute was designed to be auxiliary and not antagonistic to the living Church. It was founded for the training of lay-workers in Christian service either at home or abroad and based on inter-denominational lines. The definite aim is to train the lay student for Christian service and to associate with the Church as the one body of Christ.
>
> Third, the impression deepens as the days of the beginnings are lived over again that the great souls who realised the vision splendid of a Bible Training Institute were truly evangelical and bequeathed that true evangelicalism. An old professor once said at a Synod meeting, "I have a decided peculiarity. I think that the text-book for Bible classes ought to be the Bible." Fifty years ago this was the ideal and time has not changed it.

Some happy memories of the writer relative to the Bothwell Street complex were partaking of the good, and reasonably-priced, lunches which were enjoyed on numerous occasions in the restaurant. The standard of the food would probably never have reached the *cordon bleu* level of today's bistros and exotic eating houses but it was wholesome and, if my memory cells are working properly, the price of 2/6d comes to mind as the cost of a lunch. Because we were in Glasgow, the check-out employee would, no doubt, have asked the pre-decimal diner for *hauf-a-croon*. For the post-decimal citizens of today, this equates to 12.5 pence.

The building maintenance overheads eventually proved too high for the G.U.E.A. and it was sold to property developers. They demolished the building in 1980 and replaced it with one of the ubiquitous, ten-a-penny, office blocks which silhouette the skylines of our modern cities today.

BUT ...

As well as the sterling work we have briefly recorded in this chapter, the G.U.E.A. Directors were responsible for bringing to birth two of Glasgow's largest and most famous Mission Halls – The Tent Hall in the City Centre near Glasgow Cross and Bethany Hall in the Bridgeton area of Glasgow's East End.

Chapter Three

THE TENT HALL

I suppose that most of us have heard preachers relating the story of a little boy who had wandered too far away from his home surroundings and got lost. Standing at the roadside crying, he was approached by a friendly policeman who asked him his address. His plaintive answer was, "I don't know my address but if you take me to the cross, I can find my way home from there." This little tale could be spiritualised as far as the Tent Hall is concerned because, situated as it was, a few hundred metres from Glasgow Cross, it was the means of pointing thousands to Calvary's Cross from where the enquirers were then able to *find their way home*.

Details of the work done by the dedicated superintendents and committed workers of the Tent Hall in downtown Glasgow will never be fully known until they are revealed to us in a bonnier land than Scotland. We shall be thrilled as we hear, maybe even from the lips of a famous Carpenter from Nazareth, the myriad tales of men and women who were rescued by His unseen hand in partnership with Glasgow's Tent Hall.

Even before the Tent Hall had reached its 50th birthday, the Glasgow United Evangelistic Association was able to include the following report in its 1924 Jubilee Souvenir book :

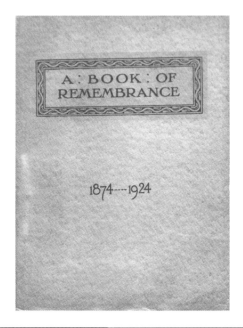

We have already referred to the transference of the work begun on Glasgow Green, in 1874, to the Tent Hall, Saltmarket, which was first known as James Morrison Street Hall. This took place in 1876. Since then this Hall has been the chief centre of the Association's Evangelistic and Ameliorative efforts.

Within its hospitable doors, which have been kept open almost continually, thousands upon thousands of human derelicts, actual and potential, have found the temporary shelter and succour which have opened the gateway through which many of them have passed to a better life and brighter lot. The work has been extensive in scope and many sided in variety, but one supreme aim has been kept in view. If the hungry have been fed, and the naked have been clothed, these things have been done, not only because they accord with the best human instincts and have the commendation of the Son of Man, but mainly as a means of bringing the poor and the social outcasts of the City within hearing of the living and life-giving message of the Gospel.

One of the positive spiritual outcomes of D.L. Moody's 1874 Mission was that a great burden to preach the Gospel to the poor had developed in the heart of Glasgow's Christian community. An evidence of this became visible to all when, after permission was granted by the City Magistrates, a large tent appeared on Glasgow Green in the summer of 1874.

The name of James Scott features largely in those early days and the archives from back then place on record that he had a *passionate zeal for the salvation of the people.*

On a Sunday morning in July 1874, Mr Scott and a few devoted helpers went to Glasgow Green to invite those who were sleeping rough into the tent to hear the Gospel message. Not too many accepted the invitation that first morning and those who did were so hungry and dejected that it was impossible to preach to them. Perhaps one of the team remembered that the Apostle James, in chapter 2 of his epistle, had written, *"If a brother or sister is poorly clothed and lacking in daily food, and one of you says to them, 'Go in peace, be warmed and filled,' without giving them the things needed for the body, what good is that?"* Anyway, it was suggested that a mug of tea and a slice of bread might be a welcome prologue to a Gospel message.

This was put into effect the following week and the *Sabbath Morning Free Breakfast for the Adult Poor* was born!

THE FREE BREAKFAST

If you ask anyone, who can recall Tent Hall days, which feature they remember most about its Evangelical outreach, the chances are that the majority will answer in three words - *The Free Breakfast*. But I wonder how many of these folks realise that, when the work was transferred from Glasgow Green to new premises at the corner of Saltmarket and Steel Street, the Free Breakfast ministry had already been in existence for about two years. The visit of D.L. Moody and Ira D. Sankey to Glasgow played a pivotal role in its early development.

The First Meal

The weather kindly provided a beautiful summer morning for the first breakfast. Some young men and women assembled in the Tent before six o'clock and, after a time of prayer, one or two remained to prepare the breakfast while the others sang *Hold the Fort* to attract the homeless folk lying on the grass into the Tent. I don't know if it was the quality of the singing or not but the immediate result was that absolutely nothing happened. The workers decided to put legs on their song by going into the highways and byways of the Green, High Street and the Bridgegate telling all and sundry that breakfast was ready. In a short space of time, more than 300 of the most degraded and destitute men and women in Glasgow entered the Tent, took breakfast and had the Gospel preached to them. They were befriended by the workers and the meeting was deemed to have been a complete success. In the following summer, as many as 1,600 were breakfasted in the Tent and as many as 2,000 were fed in the nearby Greendyke Street Drill Hall when the colder, wintry days arrived.

Four years after its inception, the Directors of the G.U.E.A. included the following paragraph regarding the Breakfast in their Annual Report :

Its object is to get in touch with drunken, homeless, destitute and depraved men and women; to hold out a helping hand to such and to encourage them to seek reformation of character and a return to honesty, industry and self-support. The meeting is Evangelistic and the food is given not only because it is right in itself to do so but because it helps Evangelism. The repast to which these people come is ours and they share it, not as paupers or inferiors, but as guests, friends and brethren.

The Sabbath Morning Free Breakfast in the Tent Hall

THE MOVE TO STEEL STREET

In 1876, the work was transferred from the Tent on Glasgow Green to a permanent venue at the corner of Saltmarket and Steel Street in the City centre. This building, which had been erected at a cost of £17,000 and had been originally known as the James Morrison Street Hall, could only be named one thing *The Tent Hall* and, for the next century plus, it became the flagship mission among Glasgow's many missions.

A Tent Hall meeting when James Haxton was Superintendent
and Peter Donald his Assistant

TIMELINE OF THE SUPERINTENDENTS

For the next century or so, the work of the Tent Hall would be headed up by various superintendents. In common with every other sphere of life, the personalities of these men varied from man to man; some were more gifted and colourful than others. I have listed below a timeline of the incumbents of the Tent Hall top job with some biographical detail. At least two of the men have had full biographies written about them and others have very little data available.

1876   James Scott

We have already featured his name a few pages back but, when the work of the Tent Hall became permanent, God had a man ready and that man was James Scott. His work had commended itself to ministers and laymen and also to Mr Moody. In 1874 the American Evangelist noted his zeal and tact and suggested him to the prayerful consideration of the G.U.E.A. Directors. Dr Andrew Bonar, in writing about him, said that, "the Lord fitted the labourer for his field of labour." Alexander Allan, of the Allan Shipping Line, was the first President of the G.U.E.A. and, when James Scott took over the reins of the Tent Hall in 1876, Mr Allan and his wife took the responsibility for Mr Scott's salary for the first two years. It is sad to record that, on 23 June 1884, James Scott died at the untimely age of 38 having spent only eight years in the new Hall.

His body was laid to rest in the Southern Necropolis in Caledonia Road in the Gorbals district of the city. It is reported that, because of the high esteem in which James Scott was held, the attendees at his funeral had to be counted in thousands, not hundreds. How apt and true the lines of the old hymn :

Shall we be missed, though by others succeeded
Reaping the fields we in springtime have sown
Yes, but the sowers must pass from their labours
Ever remembered by what they have done.

1884   John Muir

Mr Muir succeeded James Scott in 1884 and worked faithfully until he went to be with the Lord in July 1889. It is historically recorded by the G.U.E.A. that John Muir's name became a household word among the frequenters of the Hall and other needy folks whom he visited.

1889 *Two Year Gap*

After Mr Muir's death in 1889, the Tent Hall had no formally appointed superintendent but, for the following two years, the work was overseen by visiting Evangelists, students from the Bible Training Institute and several G.U.E.A. Directors. One of the Directors was a Mr James S. Napier. One of the later Superintendents said that he had a great heart of love and remembers seeing him, after the Free Breakfast, over washing the feet of some of the derelicts and weeping as he did so.

1901   Robert Logan

Mr Logan had previously been an Evangelist with the Ayrshire Christian Union and, since 1891, had been Superintendent of Bethany Hall, Bridgeton. In 1901 the G.U.E.A. transferred him to head the work in the Tent Hall and he laboured there until his resignation in 1908.

1908   P.T. McRostie

Peter McRostie was known as *the Man who Walked Backwards and* became Superintendent in 1908. Like his predecessor, Mr McRostie had been an Evangelist with Ayrshire Christian Union and he also was transferred from the Bethany Hall in Bridgeton. One of Mr McRostie's many strengths was his presentation of *lantern lectures* and the Tent Hall regulars loved the Saturday evenings when these were scheduled.

For those not familiar with this *technology*, let me explain. A device called a magic lantern – the forerunner of the slide projector – was used to project slides onto a screen. These slides were mega compared to their 35mm great-grandsons and consisted of two pieces of glass with a picture or a graphic sandwiched in between them. The lantern which did the projecting could be a fairly cumbersome device but it had the advantage that, because it generated a fair amount of watts, it helped to heat the venue on a winter's night!

Some of Mr McRostie's presentations were aimed at the demon drink and, once during the intimations, he presented the following ditty to the amused Tent Hall audience.

One evening in October,
When I was far from sober,
And carrying home a load with manly pride;
My feet began to stutter,
And I fell down in the gutter,
A pig came up and lay down by my side.
Then I warbled, 'It's fair weather
When good fellows get together,
Till a lady passing by was heard to say -
'You can tell a man who boozes
By the company he chooses,'
And the pig got up and slowly walked away.

Mr McRostie continually drove his body at full throttle and it was not surprising that, during the last few years of his life, he suffered some serious health problems. From the autumn of 1932, he became weaker and weaker, although he had a few periods of respite. The end finally came on 27 July 1933 when his spirit went into the presence of the One who, by His death, had conquered death. His public funeral service was held in the Tent Hall two days later and was taken by his friends and peers from the Mission Hall scene in Glasgow. He was interred at Eastwood Cemetery and the grave-diggers passed comment that they had never witnessed a funeral where the two ends of the social scale were so visibly and publicly represented.

Mr Troup has had a biography written detailing his life story and I will therefore only focus on the years surrounding his Tent Hall days. If you wish to know more about him, the book is titled *Revival Man* and was written by Dr George Mitchell. It is well worth a read.

Mr Troup commenced his 13 years of service in the Tent Hall as Assistant to P.T. McRostie. His first Sunday on the famous platform was on 8 October 1932. He took over the full reins in 1933 after the death of his predecessor.

His years at the Tent Hall included those of the Second World War and the work done by him in supporting and encouraging the people who had gone from the Tent Hall into active military service is still lovingly remembered.

James Haxton was appointed as Jock Troup's Assistant and became overseeing superintendent when Mr Troup went into itinerant ministry.

Jock Troup died in America on 18 April 1954. He had just begun preaching in Knox Presbyterian Church in Spokane, Washington and, as he gave out the text *Ye must be born again*, he collapsed and fell. He had often expressed a wish to his wife and friends that, "If the Lord takes me home before He comes, I hope that He will take me while preaching the Gospel." His wish was granted!

1946   James Haxton

Mr Haxton had been with the Glasgow City Mission and led their Camlachie branch in Coalhill Street for a number of years. During his time there, it was recorded they had *blessing akin to revival*. He agreed to come to the Tent Hall as Mr Troup's Assistant.

One ex-Tent-Haller informed me that Mr Haxton had a unique tradition; during the days where evening meetings were scheduled, when the Hall was empty, he would walk round the aisles and, looking at the hundreds of vacant seats, would pray for the people who would soon be sitting on them listening to the message of the Gospel.

Peter Donald, who had been assistant to Willie Climie at the Seamen's Bethel in Brown Street, was appointed as Assistant to Mr Haxton. Mr Donald told me that, for a period of more than three years, souls were counselled every single weekend following the meetings. This was attributed to the emphasis on prayer at that time. They had powerful Friday evening prayer meetings and a monthly day of prayer. Peter Donald was later appointed to be the Superintendent at Bethany Hall in Bridgeton.

Mr Haxton concluded his 1951 end-of-year message with the following verse :

> Before me is a future all unknown, a path untrod;
> Beside me is a friend, well-loved and known;
> That Friend is God.
> Before me lies a new and unseen way,
> Midst shadows dim;
> Beside me is my Guide, and day by day
> I walk with Him.

Although unknown to him, how prophetic it turned out to be because, on 15 June 1952 James Haxton was asked to preach at Hermon Baptist Church as the resident minister, James Heron, was on holiday. After the morning service, he was conducting a Communion Service when he dropped dead at the Lord's Table. Can you think of a better place to leave for Glory?

1952   John Moore

In the footsteps of Peter Donald, Mr Moore had been the assistant at the Seamen's Bethel in Brown Street. During his time there and, after ministering to a foreign seaman in a Glasgow hospital, he returned to his home in Kirkintilloch and wrote, his inspired, world-famous and multi-lingual hymn, *Burdens are Lifted at Calvary*.

John Moore's years at the Tent Hall were very fruitful and much was accomplished during his ministry. Many renowned people ministered on the famous platform and it was during this time that the 1955 All Scotland Crusade was held in the Kelvin Hall with Billy Graham and his team from the United States of America. Mr Moore left Glasgow to become the minister of the Baptist Church in Castle Street, Inverness. He now lives in Ontario, Canada.

1961   Stanley Collins

Mr Collins came to the Tent Hall from Carrubber's Close Mission on Edinburgh's Royal Mile. He was a mighty preacher of the Word and, when he eventually left, it was to take up the position of resident preacher at a Christian Holiday Centre in America.

1967   Alex Bain

Mr Bain came from the Dawson Mission in Carron, near Falkirk. Another good man although probably lacking the charisma of some of his predecessors. During his Tent Hall years, he reached retirement age and moved to Newquay in Devon.

1975   Bill Kilpatrick

Bill Kilpatrick came from the Lanarkshire area and, when he eventually moved on, he also crossed the Atlantic to pastures new.

1977   David Cassells

David Cassells was the final person to hold the title of Tent Hall Superintendent and the doors of the hallowed establishment were finally closed in April 1979.

BUT NOT FORGETTING ...

During one of my interviews with a senior *Tent Haller*, we were discussing the biographies of some superintendents when he said to me, "There is one name you must include in the story – David Tweedie." I had to admit that the name did not ring any bells in my mind. I was then informed that David had been the Caretaker of the Tent Hall for 66 years – yes, 66 years! Various superintendents came and went but David Tweedie remained! Some days after our discussions, I received a copy of the picture below, showing bread being arranged in the Tent Hall for one of the meals. The dark-suited man at the far end of the table is David Tweedie, the white-coated man, Joe Hadsley, his assistant.

I must be honest, hearing the story of the years of faithful dedication and commitment which were given by this saint gave me quite a thrill and I have no doubt that he will have many exciting experiences to share with us when we meet him in that promised and better land.

THE WEEKLY SCHEDULE

It has been said that *many Christians do nothing but there are no Christians who have nothing to do*. One of the obvious features of a visit to the Tent Hall was the bustling activity of its army of volunteer workers. Although the dedication of the superintendents was higher than high, the ministry of the Tent Hall would have been impossible without the involvement and commitment of its myriad workers – some visible but some never in the public eye.

Ena McRostie, the widow of Mr Peter McRostie, published a biography of her husband's life in 1934 and, from it, I was able to glean a lot of facts about the Tent Hall. One of the very interesting items was the amount of ongoing activity in the Steel Street venue; here is the weekly schedule :

Sunday

7.00 a.m.   First on the agenda for Sunday was a Prayer Meeting. This was followed by

8.00 a.m.   The Free Breakfast.

11.00 a.m.   Since the Tent Hall was *Church* for many of the workers, a Communion Service was convened on the first Sunday of every month to allow them to remember the Lord's death.

2.00 p.m.   The Poor Children's Dinner. While this was being held, the second Prayer Meeting of the day was taking place. This was followed by *tracting* - delivering gospel leaflets to the tenements in the surrounding area.

3.30 p.m.   A United Fellowship Meeting for the workers.

5.15 p.m.   Young People's Bible Class. While this was in progress, a United Prayer Meeting was also taking place. After prayer, two open air meetings were convened and these were followed by a public march back to the Tent Hall.

6.45 p.m.   The Poor Girls' Bible Class.

7.00 p.m.   The Gospel Service.

The Open Air at Glasgow Cross

Monday

The Junior and Senior Christian Endeavour Societies.

Tuesday

A Sewing Class for girls.

Thursday

3.00 p.m.   Women's Meeting.
7.00 p.m.   Prayer Meeting.
7.30 p.m.   Open Air.
8.00 p.m.   Gospel Service – sometimes a Testimony Meeting.

Friday

Special Night of Prayer.

Saturday

6.00 p.m.   Prayer Meeting.
6.20 p.m.   Open Air – preceded by a march up Saltmarket and along Argyle Street.
7.00 p.m.   Gospel Tea Meeting – including *Lantern Lectures* and special speakers.

When the details of the weekly activities are studied and analysed, I do not think we need to engage the services of Sherlock Holmes to determine the reason for the success and growth of the Tent Hall; I think it has everything to do with the number of times the word *Prayer* appears in their schedules.

It has often been said that the only thing we learn from history is that we do not learn anything from history. I think that phrase is very apposite in this context and, if we want to see God move again in our Land and our Fellowships, we already know the key to achieve our objective.

THE FESTIVE SEASON

In addition to the Tent Hall's *normal* weekly schedule, other events were organised during the year and especially during the Christmas and New Year period.

To give a flavour of historical times, the following pages show some details from Tent Hall programmes dating back to 1925 :

In his introduction to the 1925 Festive events programme Mr McRostie includes the following report :

For us, the past year has been a time of perpetual blessing. The numbers of people coming to hear the Gospel have been well maintained and have sometimes been more than we could accommodate and there has been a steady flow of men and women, and lads and girls seeking to know the way of salvation. Not a few of these have been young men who, we feel sure, will make splendid workers in the future. It has been a great joy to us to watch the progress of the Young People's Bible Class conducted by Mr R.C. Brown. If we had nothing but this Class in the Tent Hall, it would be worthwhile. It is a matter for thanksgiving to see as many as 350 young men and women in the Back Hall at 5.15 on Sunday afternoons drinking in the precious truth of the Word of God.

There then followed pages advertising a Hogmanay Supper, Watch Night Service, New Year Soiree and many other events.

From the design on the front of the programme, it is easy to deduce that Britain was at war during this period; however, from the list of events inside the document, it is equally easy to see, as far as the ministry of the Tent Hall was concerned that, because of the wartime conditions, it was not a case of *business as usual* but *more business than usual*!

The 1941/42 programme contained an alphabetical list of 213 names of those serving with His Majesty's Forces to whom Mr Troup's weekly mail letter was sent.

The graphic on the following page is a facsimile of one of the pages from the 1941 programme showing that the Tent Hall ministry during the war was not only supporting young folk who had gone *from* Glasgow to help in the war effort but to young folk who had come *to* Glasgow for the same purpose.

The statistics shown on the page give some idea as to the scale of the project.

SERVICES WITH H.M. FORCES

SATURDAY at 6 p.m.

SUNDAY 7 p.m.

We commenced this work amongst the Men of H.M. Forces just over one year ago; 14,000 have been provided with free meals, but best of all, about 300 of these dear boys have made a definite decision for Christ. This work has meant much extra labour and expense, the labour is done mostly by our noble band of voluntary workers who contact the men on the streets and invite them to tea by means of an invitation card. Men from all the allied countries, and also from every part of the Empire have been our guests as we seek to carry out the scriptural injunction "Extend ungrudging hospitality toward one another" (Wey.).

The front page of the 1951 Festive schedule of events shows a normal *respectable* congregation leaving the Tent Hall, maybe after the Saturday at Seven meeting. However, on page 5 of the programme, we see examples of the people that the Tent Hall workers *loved* to see in the congregations. They are maybe not as well *turned out* as those in the cover picture but they are equally part of the *other sheep* of whom Jesus Christ said "them also I must bring."

The work done by the Tent Hall in preaching the Gospel to the poor in Glasgow was tremendous but the work done in feeding the poor was equally tremendous. One of the events of the Festive Season was the *Annual Hogmanay Supper to the Aged Poor*.

During my research, I was shown an actual copy of an historical shopping list for this Supper; the figures are quite mind-boggling :

Loaves of Bread	1,000
Steak Pies	1,000
Sultana Cakes	80 x 6lb (2.7 Kg)
Sugar	Half a Ton (508 Kg)
Tea	250lb (113.6 Kg)

Back in those days there were no ASDA, Tesco or Sainsbury stores offering their *Buy One – Get One Free* deals so the cost of hosting these events must have been quite prohibitive. But maybe not – because God was involved!

The picture below is an advert regarding one of these Suppers.

Friday, 26th December—7.30 p.m.

ANNUAL HOGMANAY SUPPER TO AGED POOR

Chairman: JAMES ROBERTSON, M.B.E., B.L., Assistant Chief Constable, Glasgow Police Force

Speakers: Rev. GEORGE A. YOUNG, EDWIN LEWIS, Rev. DONALD STUART

Others taking part: G. HOOD, P. DONALD, A. STEWART, J. M. MOORE

Song Ministry: "MALE VOICE TRIO", JOHN SILCOCK, and FREE BREAKFAST CHOIR.

Admission by Ticket Only

No one under 16 years can be admitted owing to the demand for tickets.

GLASGOW UNITED EVANGELISTIC ASSOCIATION

TENT HALL

STEEL STREET, SALTMARKET, GLASGOW, C.1.

Superintendent — — — — — MR. ALEXANDER S. BAIN
Organist: MR. ROBERT CHRISTIE. *Pianist*: MRS. JOHN ALLAN.
Choir Leaders: MR. THOMAS GRAY AND MR. ROBERT J. CLARKE.
Recording Engineers: MR. JOHN McCRAE AND MR. ANDREW CARTER.

WEEKLY PROGRAMME

SUNDAY	PRAYER MEETING .... — — — — —	7 a.m.
	FREE BREAKFAST SERVICE — — —	8 a.m.
	BIBLE SCHOOL FOR ALL AGES — — —	10 a.m.
	SUNDAY SCHOOL — — — — —	2 p.m.
	BACK COURT WORK — — — —	2.30 p.m.
	SPIRITUAL TONIC SERVICE — — —	3.30 p.m.
	PRAYER MEETING — — — —	5.15 p.m.
	OPEN-AIR MEETING: ALBION STREET — —	6 p.m.
	EVANGELISTIC SERVICE — — — —	7 p.m.
	HOSPITAL FELLOWSHIP: meets at Baird Street — —	7 p.m.
MONDAY	NOON MEETING IN THE CHRISTIAN INSTITUTE — —	12 noon
	YOUNG PEOPLE'S FELLOWSHIP — — —	7.30 p.m.
TUESDAY	PRAYER MEETING — — — — —	7 p.m.
	YOUNG LADIES' SEWING CLASS — .... —	7.30 p.m.
	FELLOWSHIP MEETING — — — —	7.45 p.m.
WEDNESDAY	HOSPITAL FELLOWSHIP: meets at Robroyston Hospital	7 p.m.
THURSDAY	WOMEN'S OWN — — — — —	2.30 p.m.
	PRAYER MEETING — — — —	7 p.m.
	MID-WEEK SERVICE — — — —	7.45 p.m.
FRIDAY	PRAYER MEETING — — — —	7.30 p.m.
SATURDAY	PRAYER MEETING — — — —	6 p.m.
	OPEN AIR MEETING—BRIDGEGATE — —	6.30 p.m.
	THE EVANGELISTIC RALLY — — —	7 p.m.

MISSIONARY PRAYER MEETING (Second Monday in Month) —	7.45 p.m.
YOUNG PEOPLE'S TRACT BAND (Alternate Saturdays) — —	3 p.m.
SENIOR CHOIR PRACTICE—Sunday — — — —	6 p.m.
JUNIOR CHOIR PRACTICE—Sunday — — — —	6 p.m.
OPEN AIR MEETING AT ALBION STREET—Sunday — —	8.45 p.m.

The graphic above is a copy of the back page of the 1967/68 Christmas and New Year Programme showing the weekly activity in the Tent Hall. If we compare it to the schedule shown earlier in this chapter during P.T. McRostie's watch, we can see that an emphasis on prayer was still very much in evidence. It is also interesting to note that the Tuesday Sewing Class had spanned the 4 decade gap!

MEMORIES

Here are a couple of memories from the Tent Hall era – the first from Peter Donald, the second from John Moore.

Lady So-and-So

One of the workers in the Tent Hall had previously been the manager of the King's Theatre in Bath Street and, while there, he had escorted some of the rich and famous from their Rolls Royce at the front door to their specially selected seats in the theatre. Among them had been, let's call her, Lady *So-and-So*.

Many years later, the same worker saw a woman, with one eye gouged out, coming into the Tent Hall in a visible state of penury but moving with a very prim gait. On closer investigation, he found that it was the same lady he had, in better times, shown to her exclusive seat in the King's Theatre. She had become a street prostitute and was reduced to being a resident in the nearby Salvation Army boarding house. She became a regular attendee at the Free Breakfast on a Sunday morning.

Sadly, sometime later she was knocked down by one of Glasgow's silent trolley buses and ended up in the Royal Infirmary. However, it is good to report that, before she died, Peter Donald had the privilege of leading her to Christ at her hospital bedside.

Matthew Francis

In the 1950s, a man by the name of Matthew Francis had been booked for a month of special services in the Tent Hall. Mr Francis hailed from a church in the North of England and was, by all accounts, a great preacher. He also used to sing solos as part of his ministry.

On his second Saturday in Glasgow, he presented a powerful message and his solo for the night was the old hymn whose verses end with the phrase : *and the toils of the road will seem nothing, when we get to the end of the way*. He repeated this refrain 5 times and asked the congregation to join him in the singing. He preached for almost an hour and, as he was coming to the end of his message, his face turned ashen white and he asked John Moore, the Superintendent, to close the meeting.

John went to the podium and proceeded to bring the meeting to an end and was completely unaware of a drama that was unfolding behind him. Mr Francis had sat down on the chairman's seat and, turning to the singers and others who had taken part in the evening's events, said to them individually, "Good bye. I'm going." He then sat back in his seat and immediately entered the presence of the Lord.
Mr Moore, oblivious to the fact that Mr Francis had just stepped from the Tent Hall platform into Heaven, gave an invitation and some people responded. He told them to make their way to the Back Hall to meet with the waiting counsellors. He then hurried off the platform and into the counselling area. He had hardly arrived there when his Assistant, Victor Whyte, came running to him and said, "John, Mr Francis has just died on the platform." The Superintendent rushed back to the platform via the kitchen and, when he got there, a distraught Mrs Francis was in tears beside her husband.

The following morning, in the Renfrewshire town of Kilmacolm, the Cook family, who owned a Grocery business in the town, had started a normal Sunday. The two sisters, Dorothy and Margaret were lying in bed reading the Sunday papers. The previous night's events in the Tent Hall were given fair coverage along with pictures which the newspaper photographers had taken about 12/13 hours ago in the Glasgow venue. The stories told of the sudden death of Mr Francis and that the Saturday evening rallies in the Tent Hall often attracted audiences of up to 2,000. This fact caught the attention of the Cook sisters and it was decided there and then that they would attend the meeting on the following Saturday. Margaret Cook was a lawyer and her sister Dorothy was involved in the family business but she was searching for that missing *something* in her life.

The next Saturday, Margaret and Dorothy Cook found themselves in the Tent Hall. The events of the previous week had ensured that it was a *standing room only* scenario with people even sitting in the windows of the top gallery. During the week, John Moore had attended and spoken at Mr Francis' funeral in England. He had been accompanied by his close friend David McNee who had sung at the service. Mr Moore took the text on which Mr Francis had been preaching and, at the end, he gave an invitation for salvation. Among those who went to the counselling room were the two Cook sisters from Kilmacolm.

As they exited from the room, Dorothy had a radiant complexion and a beautiful smile on her face. John Moore asked her what had happened. She replied, "I came alive tonight", and her sister Margaret agreed.

Within a year, Dorothy had enrolled at the Bible Training Institute in Bothwell Street and, after graduation, she went to Cyprus as a missionary with the Mission to Mediterranean Garrisons and, working among the soldiers, sailors and airmen, led many of them to her Saviour.

By strange co-incidence, the Lord took Dorothy to be with Himself as suddenly as He had taken Matthew Francis, the man who started it all by dying on the Tent Hall platform.

THE ROMANCE OF GLASGOW'S TENT HALL

The words that have been written on the previous pages regarding the ministry of the Tent Hall are but a zillionth of what could have been said and, of course, they only cover people and events that are known. During its years of activity there were hundreds of thousands of encounters in tenements and closes, streets and back-courts which, to this day, are humanly unknown and unrecorded.

This final section was originally titled *The Epitaph* but, because epitaphs are, by nature, sad, I did not want to leave you with that emotion regarding the Tent Hall. I have therefore culled a headline from an article in *The Christian* magazine dated December 9, 1949. When we think of the word *Romance* it usually evokes connotations of love, which is very appropriate for our subject, but the Cambridge Dictionary provides another meaning when it defines the word as *a story of exciting events especially set in the past*; hence my new title fits exactly!

The Tent Hall was one of the greatest institutions that Glasgow has ever known; not because of its architecture but because of what happened within its architecture. This was a tribute paid by someone on its 50th anniversary.

While the Tent Hall has ever had an open door for the poor and needy who have repaired to it of their own accord, whether for the alleviation of temporal distress or for the appeasement of the hunger which afflicts the soul, the work has been pre-eminently aggressive. It has been a veritable going out "into the streets and lanes of the City" – to those who are so sunk in sin or so indifferent that they have had no desire to come, and compelling them to come in. Open-air and back-court services and extensive visitation from house to house have therefore been prominent features of the methods employed in all seasons and in all kinds of

> weather. By such means, many who might otherwise have been left to drift or to sink, have had the Gospel life-line thrown out to them and, grasping it, have been rescued from making shipwreck of their lives.

Is it possible to discover a reason for the success of the century of successful Evangelism which the Tent Hall experienced? Surely there must be a logical explanation which can help us think about what we can do today to reach the same heights and depths of spiritual attainment.

In 1949, Rev. Thomas Cameron engaged in an investigation to find answers to these very questions and he wrote about it as follows :

> The secret of this centre of spiritual life lies neither in the Saturday nor Sunday night meetings, nor yet at the Free Breakfast. It is to be found elsewhere, and I was privileged to see it. Guided by the Superintendent, who opened a door and ushered me into a small room, I found myself in the presence of 120 men and women on their knees for two whole hours, wrestling in prayer for blessing upon their work and for the conversion of sinners. It was a Friday evening in the midst of summer, when most Church agencies are suspended. For those faithful people, prayer suffers no suspension. Nor were their prayers brief or faulty. They were the utterances of men and women consecrated for service, convinced of the efficacy of prayer and the certainty of its being answered. I recollected that the number was exactly the same as of the Upper Room Company at the time of Pentecost.

I'm sure as you read Mr Cameron's words, like me, it was probably what you expected to read because, deep down we all know that any advance in God's kingdom is always – and only – via His time-tested and non-negotiable method of prayer.

As we come to the end of our thoughts and reminiscences of this legendary Glasgow establishment, let me close with a paragraph which was written by a visitor to the venue in its heyday :

> A visit to the Tent Hall is like touring a well equipped factory, stocked with all the latest accessories, down to the great ton-weight urn capable of holding 8,500 cups of tea. The floors are as spotlessly clean as in a royal household, and the work is organised efficiently and economically.

He then concludes by saying :

> Glasgow has good reason to be proud of its Tent Hall.

And who will dare argue with that statement?

Chapter Four

BETHANY HALL

If you start at Glasgow Cross and proceed eastward along London Road, you will, within a few hundred metres, come to a building on your left bearing a sign saying *Barrowland*. Known by the city dwellers as *The Barras*, this is Glasgow's equivalent to London's Portobello Road and, although the marketing techniques are maybe comparable, the London street market cannot boast of having the Glasgow *patter*. This is guaranteed to liven up the selling process and, at the same time, provide much entertainment to the bemused bystanders.

Proceeding further along London Road will take you through the Calton district and, having passed the old Templeton carpet factory on the right-hand side, not far from the famous People's Palace on Glasgow Green, you will arrive at downtown Bridgeton. Turning right at the Cross brings you into Main Street and the first opening on the left is Muslin Street; this was the final address of the Bethany Hall but it had two previous locations before arriving there.

BRIDGETON

I don't know if it is a function of city planners nationwide or just a geographical co-incidence but it seems that, in many cities, the *West Ends* contain the leafy suburbs and big houses while the *East Ends* contain the poorer members of society with housing and social conditions to match. Bridgeton is in the East End!

Like much of Glasgow today, the Bridgeton district shows clear evidence of urban renewal and a drive through its streets and roads can be confusing to expatriate Glaswegians returning to the city and attempting to indulge in a nostalgic pilgrimage of their roots. In the late 19th century it was a very different story. The district was predominantly populated by traditional Glasgow tenements. These were large sandstone buildings divided into separate flats. Entrance into the flats was made by the *close* – a *wally* close if you were posh! The close was a passage allowing access to the stairs and also to the back courts where the family laundry could be hung out to dry on pre-determined days – right next to the garbage bins of course!

Compared to today, conditions were archaic. Large families were the order of the day and, if someone decided they *needed* a bath, a journey had to be made to the nearest *baths* – swimming pools or leisure centres in modern lingo. Sanitation standards were extremely primitive and one of the results was the infamous *stair-head lavatories*. One Christian friend who regularly climbed the tenement stairs while delivering tracts to the residents has strong nasal memories of these facilities; part of a verse in the Gospel of John springs to mind and seems appropriate, *"and the house was filled with the odour …"*

IN THE BEGINNING …

The very successful Campaign by Moody and Sankey in 1874 on Glasgow Green resulted in a resolution being passed by the Directors of the Glasgow United Evangelistic Association.

Let me quote from their 1924 Jubilee Souvenir publication
A Book of Remembrance:

The special needs of the East-end of the City were early laid on the hearts of the Directors, and the Association's work there was begun in a hall in Sister Street, Bridgeton, in 1875. The following year it was transferred to Bethany Hall, Bernard Street, through the good offices of the late Mr James S. Napier, who generously gifted it to the Association in 1903, with the stipulation that his name should not appear in any Minute or Report as the donor.

Bernard Street is situated east of Bridgeton Cross and runs parallel to London Road. It is only a few hundred metres from the modern stadium complex of Celtic Football Club.

Bethany Hall was situated on the north side of Bernard Street between Dunn Street and Boden Street. The main hall, which included a gallery, could seat 1,500 people.

THE SUPERINTENDENTS

The following men served as superintendents of the Bethany Hall. They are listed in chronological order.

Walter S. Hislop

Mr Hislop was charged with the responsibility of the work from the early days. He had received a positive spiritual experience during the 1874 Moody Sankey Mission and, as a result of that, spent the rest of his short life in serving his Bridgeton parishioners by seeking to ensure their salvation. Sadly, he died in 1884, having not even reached half of the Biblical three score and ten years.

William Ralston

Mr Ralston, one of the G.U.E.A. Directors, picked up Mr Hislop's baton and continued the race with great zeal and devotion until he also went to be with the Lord seven years later in 1891.

Robert Logan

The next Superintendent was Mr Robert Logan, an evangelist with the Ayrshire Christian Union. He accepted the invitation to come to Bethany Hall and gave unstinting service and energy to his calling.

It is recorded that Robert Logan was a great organiser and motivator of people. Statistics for 1898 reflect the activity of the Bethany Hall under his leadership :

Prayer Meetings	270
Open Air Gatherings	510
Indoor Meetings	766
Attendees at services	over 167,000
Visits to homes in the district	over 100,000

Not a bad year's effort for a Mission Hall in the East End of Glasgow! Mr Logan was transferred by the G.U.E.A. to the Tent Hall in 1901.

Peter T. McRostie

Another Ayrshire Christian Union evangelist was next on the list for Bethany Hall. Affectionately known as *the man who walked backwards*, Mr McRostie led the work for seven years when, like his predecessor, he was transferred to the Tent Hall; that was in 1908.

Robert Millar

Incumbent number five was Mr Robert Millar. He had been a Missionary connected to Finnieston United Free Church and he served Bethany Hall for seventeen years. For most of his Bethany years he was helped by Mr Sinclair McLeod as Visiting Assistant. Mr Millar left the Bethany Hall to take up a position at Carrubbers Close Mission, situated on Edinburgh's famous Royal Mile near John Knox's house. This Mission was another visible landmark on the Scottish skyline as a result of the visit to the country of Dwight L. Moody and Ira D. Sankey.

Walter Millar

Before coming to Bethany Hall, Mr Millar was superintendent at the Canal Boatmen's Institute in Port Dundas Road. He took over the work at Bridgeton early in 1925.

We can be specific about his start date because his grandson, Gordon Haxton has in his possession the Young's Analytical Concordance which was presented to Mr Millar when he left the Canal Boatmen's Institute. This book is inscribed with the date of 8 January 1925 and it would be immediately after this that he came to Bethany. He remained in the Bethany Hall for approximately thirteen years.

Edward Spence

Detailed history seems to be rather scarce regarding Mr Edward Spence. The Orkney Islands have been mentioned as a possible source for his roots but, as to where he went after Bethany, I have not been able to ascertain. What is remembered is that his time in Bridgeton was relatively short.

Neil Taylor

Mr Taylor had been the assistant superintendent under Walter Millar and he was appointed leader after Edward Spence left. His family roots were in the Falkirk area and his service at Bridgeton encountered some difficult days. The Second World War was in progress and many of the young men and women from the area were called up for active service. One very famous citizen of Glasgow said, "At the tender age of eighteen, I felt the call of the sea, or as it was then known – *conscription"*

The long winter evenings were subject to *black-out* restrictions and travel to the evening services therefore became difficult for some people and impossible for others.

During Mr Taylor's reign, major structural alterations were made to the Bernard Street premises. A new floor level was added and what had formerly been the *gallery* became the *small hall upstairs*. The superintendent eventually went into full-time ministry with one of the denominational churches.

Willie McCracken

William McCracken was previously an Evangelist with the Lanarkshire Christian Union and he came to Bethany Hall around the time that the war ended. In fact, a special event was arranged to welcome back all the men and women who had served in the forces.

He was an encourager, a great man of prayer and had a burden for souls. As a result, extended and all night prayer meetings were features of his days at Bernard Street.

During his term as superintendent, he invited a number of Irish evangelists to hold campaigns in Bethany Hall.

In more recent times, Mr McCracken's grandson – Craig Dyer – was a pastor of Harper Memorial Church in the Plantation area of the city.

Annie Darroch

For many years, the Bethany Hall had a *Bible Woman* who was responsible for leading the women's work and visitation. Two previous holders of this post were Miss Waugh and Miss Jack.

During the early days of Mr McCracken's leadership, a lady from Port Charlotte on the island of Islay arrived to fill the *Bible Woman* slot. She was always known simply as *Miss Darroch*. She had been a Faith Mission Pilgrim for many years and continued to don the Mission's traditional bonnet which she said, "opened doors" during her visitation work.

Miss Darroch spoke with a strong Scottish *island* accent and was very much given to prayer. She stayed at Bethany through to the Muslin Street years and left a deep imprint on the life of the Bridgeton Mission.

Miss A. Darroch

Charlie Main

Charlie Main came from a fishing family in Dunbar, East Lothian. His temperament was in complete contrast to his predecessor. Mr McCracken was of a more serious disposition but Charlie was one of life's *colourful characters*! He was an old soldier who "fought in Kitchener's Army" and had become an Army Scripture Reader.

Shortly after his arrival at Bethany, he held a series of Bible Teaching meetings on the subject of *Ages before Moses*. It was obviously based on the book of Genesis and they were apparently quite memorable meetings.

Charlie came to Bridgeton around 1949/1950 but left after a few years because he was an evangelist at heart and wanted to return to itinerant preaching.

Peter Donald

The next move bucked the historical trend because, up till this point, all personnel transfers had been *westward* in direction, from the Bethany Hall to the Tent Hall, this one was *eastward* from the Tent Hall to the Bethany Hall.

James Haxton was the Tent Hall Superintendent and, after Charlie Main left, the G.U.E.A. asked his Assistant, Peter Donald, to take the leading role at the Bethany Hall. Peter arrived there in 1951. Co-incidental with this, John Moore moved from the Seamen's Chapel, in Brown Street, to be the new assistant at the Tent Hall.

Peter was of a milder disposition and an extremely gracious man, a very gifted musician and a great encourager of others. His wife, Betty, was a lovely person too and they won the respect of many during their Bethany years.

Peter remained in the Bethany Hall until 1957 when the Harper Memorial Baptist Church, situated in the city's Plantation district, called him to be their minister.

George Bell

George Bell had moved in and out of the Glasgow Mission scene over the years. He had been assistant superintendent at the Tent Hall prior to Peter Donald and James Haxton, the superintendent, thought highly of him. He was a man of prayer and prophetic preaching. He had moved back into a preaching ministry for a period but was invited to succeed Peter Donald at Bethany, which he did.

It was during his leadership that the G.U.E.A. announced that, for financial reasons, they were no longer able to maintain the work in Bernard Street and a closing date was given.

There was a good nucleus of workers in Bethany who were keen to continue the witness in Bridgeton and George was supportive of this. However, he did say that, whilst he would see the changeover through, he would not continue as superintendent.

THE WEEKLY SCHEDULE

Like most of the other Mission Halls in Glasgow, Bethany Hall was a weekly hive of activity.

Sunday

Sundays kicked off with a morning Worship Service and then, at 11 o'clock, hundreds of local children gathered for the Children's Meeting.

This was not like a traditional Sunday School where, after some singing, the children split into classes. Everyone stayed together and, after the preliminaries, the kids would listen to a preacher with a practical object lesson to help them remember the story. One man who remembers attending these gatherings told me that they made a profound impression on his young life.

Sunday afternoons hosted the Men's Meeting. This was an extremely successful outreach and for many years saw attendances of up to 600 men being presented with the claims of Christ.

The final activity for Sunday was an evening Gospel Service.

Tuesday

Tuesday evenings were set aside for the Fellowship Meeting. The focus of this gathering was Bible Teaching and, over the years, many visiting speakers made their way to Bridgeton to edify the saints through the teaching of God's Word.

Wednesday

The Mission doors opened again on Wednesday afternoon – this time for the Women's Meeting. Through the years, this was very well attended and supported.

Thursday

In these modern 21st century days, when it is difficult to get unsaved people into a Gospel Service on a Sunday evening, it seems strange to report that Bethany Hall managed to get them in on a Thursday evening as well. A mid-week Gospel Service!

Friday

When the congregation arrived at the door for the Friday evening meeting, they were handed a copy of the Redemption Songs and a kneeling mat – this was Prayer Meeting night!

In the later years, when the demographic changes began to kick in and the Bridgeton population were being moved to other areas, the Friday evening service was merged with the Thursday evening service.

Saturday

For many citizens in Bridgeton, Saturdays always seemed slow in arriving. Why? It was *Tea Meeting* night in Bethany Hall! This type of meeting was not unique to Bethany but was a popular event in the Glasgow Mission scene generally. Many of the folk had to work long hours during the week to try to balance the housekeeping debits and credits and, having attempted do so, they could eagerly anticipate the warmth, welcome and fellowship they would find at the Saturday Tea Meetings.

The programmes were bright and well organised and were presented by visiting *deputations*. I'm not sure if this word, in this context, is unique to Central Scotland but it meant that a group of people had travelled from another fellowship and probably another town or area to present a programme to the gathered audience. The programme could range from *normal* items like solos, groups, choirs and speakers to *not so normal* items like someone playing percussion on a set of spoons or someone pulling a violin bow over the teeth of a carpenter's saw, creating the most dreadful sounds ever heard by the human ear while euphemistically introducing it as *the musical saw*.

But of course you can't have a Tea Meeting without tea and this was part of the attraction of being in Bridgeton on a Saturday evening. Speaking of the beverage on offer at Bethany Hall, Charlie Clark used to comment that, "the tea was great – everybody got a slice."

A memorable feature of these evenings was the inclusion in the programme of testimonies of men and women whose lives had been transformed by the grace of God. These folk were visible and living proof of the power of the Gospel of Jesus Christ. Many of them had literally been rescued from the gutter of sin and were able to share how that the Good Shepherd had searched diligently for the missing 100th sheep and had not given up – "*until He found it.*"

FAREWELL BERNARD STREET

The Right Hon. Lord Maclay, P.C. LL.D. of Kilmacolm was a great help to the Glasgow Missions and, if there was a financial need, he was prepared to meet it. His Lordship was a wealthy ship owner and lived at Duchal Castle in Inverclyde.

When Walter Millar was in charge at Bernard Street and his good friend Jock Troup was Superintendent at the Tent Hall in Steel Street, they would sometimes get a telephone call from Lord Maclay's secretary inviting them to come down to his home for the day. They would board a train at the old St Enoch railway station and, on arrival at Bridge of Weir, the company chauffeur was on hand to transport them to the castle.

Lord Maclay would then ask if they needed new seats at the Tent Hall or new hymn books at Bethany Hall and if they did, his cheque book was always available and open. But, in spite of benevolent men like Lord Maclay, financial constraints were becoming necessary and, after the deaths of Lord Maclay and other prominent business men, the G.U.E.A. decided to close the Hall in Bernard Street.

However, there was a group of workers who felt the burden to continue the work and a new door opened up to them.

HELLO MUSLIN STREET

About half a mile away from Bernard Street, in Muslin Street, there was a branch of Y.W.C.A. Scotland. Through the kindness of the ladies on the local committee, a ground floor hall, which was not in use, was made available on a rental basis to the Bethany workers.

Part of a congregation in the 1960s

An eight-man committee consisting of Willie McKinstry, Archie McKinstry, Willie Thompson, David McPhee, Willie Carrick, Dick Dickson, David Haxton and Gordon Haxton was formed to oversee and lead the work. Much physical work required to be done to renovate the place but *where there's a will ...* - and willing workers - the job gets done! One of the tasks in the project was to adjust the length of some of the old wooden seats from Bernard Street and transport them to Muslin Street. After much toil and sweat, the work re-opened there in 1959;

THE FESTIVE SEASON

In similar fashion to the Tent Hall and other Missions, Bethany Hall arranged a comprehensive schedule of events over the annual Christmas and New Year period and, looking over previous year's programmes, recalls some cherished memories and reveals some interesting facts.

The graphic above is a page from the 1963-64 Festive Programme but is typical of other years as well. I selected this one for two reasons :

Firstly, it shows a picture of Mrs Bessie Sykes who was a living legend in her time and was also, along with her husband Seth, the writers of *Thank You Lord for Saving My Soul*, a chorus which has now travelled to the uttermost parts of the world.

Secondly, the advert for the Gospel Tea Meeting on Saturday 4th January shows that the singers were the Kilsyth Young Ladies Group; one of the *Young* Ladies of that Group has been my wife now for half a century.

One of the features of Bethany Hall programmes was that, no matter who the visiting deputation singers were, there were slots made available in the order of service for one or more of the Bethany choirs to sing and there were four choir variations to select from – Senior, Women's, Male Voice and Junior.

The picture above shows the Senior Choir in full flight under the baton of Willie McKinstry and the picture below is a posed shot of the Junior Choir in the 1960s with their conductor Dick Dickson.

On the 1964-65 programme there was a picture of a young male soloist called David McNee. In later years this young man became Commissioner of the Metropolitan Police in London and also became Sir David McNee.

THE CURTAIN FINALLY FALLS

There were some good and fruitful years in Muslin Street and many people were saved.

Campaigns were held and visiting evangelists included John Wesley White - one of Billy Graham's Associate Evangelists. The Youth for Christ organisation also evangelised and, among the more famous of their personnel were the

Palermo Brothers. Louis and Phil Palermo were musical evangelists who began their ministry in 1938 with the Chicago Midnight Brigade and were involved worldwide with Youth for Christ right up to 1982.

However, Bridgeton was a-changing - or rather being changed. Major development work was set in motion to rid the district of the housing deprivation and associated social problems. To facilitate this process, the local population were being decanted to districts like Blairdardie, East Kilbride and Cumbernauld, the latter two being members of Scotland's growing club of *New Towns*.

In 1971 things eventually came to the point where it was becoming a life-support situation and the overseeing brethren decided it would be better for the remaining members of the congregation to move into Christian fellowships in their local communities. However, a small group of stalwarts, mainly of an older age group were reluctant to accept the closure and carried on valiantly for a few more years.

MEMORIES

Here are three memories from Bethany Hall days.

Sinclair McLeod

A Bethany Hall open air meeting was in progress at the corner of London Road and Dunn Street and a man called Sinclair McLeod was preaching. Sinclair had been a real rough diamond but he was now an ardent soul winner for his Lord. During the course of his message, a man standing in the ring came towards him and shouted, "Away wi' yer Christ" and spat in his face. Mr McLeod wiped the spittle from his face and carried on preaching.

Some months later, while a service was in progress in Bethany Hall, a message was delivered to the door requesting that Sinclair McLeod go immediately to a certain address in Nuneaton Street – two streets along Bernard Street. True to his character and calling, Sinclair made his way to the address not knowing who was expecting him. He knocked the door and was shown into the room. It was a typical Glasgow tenement building with its *set-in* beds and on one of the beds, an obviously ill man was lying. He asked Mr McLeod, "Do you know me?" and, when the visitor answered that he didn't, the patient in the bed continued, "Well I'm the man that spat in your face and said 'Away wi' yer Christ' – but I need Him now".

Sinclair McLeod had the joy of leading yet another soul to his Lord.

Tommy Hamilton

Tommy Hamilton was a stage comedian in the old music hall days playing alongside stars like Will Fyfe and Dave Willis. He lived in a house in Loretto Street, Carntyne on the opposite side of the street from the Haxton family. One winter morning, just after the New Year - January 4 to be precise, - the telephone rang in the Haxton home and a voice said, 'Is that you Davie?', Mr Haxton said, 'Yes' and the caller, Tommy Hamilton said, 'I'm in trouble, could you come across and see me?'

When David Haxton entered the house it was obvious that Tommy was very much the worse of alcohol. Because of his condition, his wife had left him and his family had lost respect for him. To crown it all he had fallen down a flight of stone stairs and had hurt himself badly. David helped him, prayed with him and told him that Michael Perrott, an Evangelist from Dublin, was finishing a special Gospel Mission in Bethany Hall that night. He invited Tommy to come and hear Mr Perrott, he agreed and was picked up and taken to Muslin Street.

Mr Perrott did not make any public appeal that night but, Gordon Haxton recalls that, during the singing of the closing hymn, he saw a little man dropping onto his knees - it was Tommy Hamilton. After the meeting, he went into the vestry with the Evangelist and got right with God. He became a wonderful trophy of Grace. His wife eventually got saved too and his family regained respect for him.

During his music hall days, Tommy had written a lot of ditties and he transferred this talent into his spiritual life. He wrote quite a number of choruses but the one that is remembered best of all is :

Wonderful, wonderful Saviour
Wonderful, wonderful Friend
Wonderful, wonderful friendship
A friendship that never will end
He is my constant Companion
We never live apart
I've got this wonderful Saviour
I've got Him right in my heart.

Jimmy Owen

Jimmy Owen was a carter by trade and part of his job was to deliver sawdust to the public houses in the Bridgeton area by horse and cart. His custom was to have a drink in every establishment he visited and, by the time he completed his deliveries, he was very drunk, or in Glasgow parlance, – *steamin'*. He commented that it was helpful that the horse knew the way back home – otherwise he would never have made it!

Before he became a Christian, he was a gambling man. One day, his wife bought two tickets for a Bethany Hall social and, "to keep the peace", Jimmy went along but he was uneasy during the service. Was the Holy Spirit convicting him of sin? Well, maybe, but the main reason was because of a bet he had placed. Gambling was illegal in those days and it was necessary to have a clandestine meeting with a bookie – probably in one of the tenement *closes* - and place your bet with him. If your horse or dog won, you had to arrange another secret meeting and collect your winnings. On the day of the social, Jimmy's horse had come in and he had won the princely sum of 3/9d. In pre-decimal Scotland, this was referred to as *three and ninepence*; in our currency today it is less than 20 pence.

As soon as the final *Amen* was pronounced, Jimmy made for the exit door but at the door stood Sinclair McLeod – a soul-winner and a *buttonholer*. Sinclair shook hands with Jimmy and the dialogue went something like this :

Sinclair : "You're a visitor here, are you a Christian?"
Jimmy : "Naw, but I'll be back on Setterday!"
Sinclair : "Ye might be deid by Setterday"

This got to Jimmy and he waited behind and committed his life to Christ. In later years, when giving his testimony, Jimmy would tell the folks that the bookie still had his 3/9d!

The famous 50 foot high "Umbrella" at Bridgeton Cross in days gone by.

An early (1930s ?) Children's Meeting in the Bernard Street Hall

A "Welcome Home" service in late 1945 or early 1946
for those who had been engaged in military service during the war;
(Some spouses and sweethearts also in the picture.)

76

Chapter Five

CANAL BOATMEN'S

During the late 18th and early 19th centuries Great Britain was in the forefront of the Industrial Revolution and it produced a radical effect on Glasgow and its environs. Some areas of the country, like Lancashire and Yorkshire, secured the cotton and rag trade industries and the city of Dundee acquired the jute market. Glasgow, probably for reasons of geology as well as geography, found that she had been assigned the *heavy industry* portfolio.

Heavy industry meant that heavy goods needed to be moved across the country. However, as motorways and Leyland Trucks had not yet become ideas in designers' minds, the concept of floating heavy goods on water seemed an obvious option for consideration. God used an awful lot of the H2O stuff in His Creation model but mainly in ocean, sea and river formats – none of which would help get heavy goods moved from Possilpark to Falkirk in 1760!

Solution to the problem? Construct a *man-made river* and call it the *Forth and Clyde Canal.*

PORT DUNDAS

The work to build the Forth and Clyde Canal started at the *Forth* end on 10 June 1768. The project took 22 years to complete and the first vessel sailed the 35 miles from Grangemouth to Bowling on 31 August 1790 – navigating 39 locks in the process. The canal flowed through the northern suburbs of Glasgow and soon played an active and important role in the city's contribution to the Industrial Revolution.

Between 1786 and 1790, a branch was cut from the main canal at Hamiltonhill to a new basin on One Hundred Acre Hill high above the burgeoning city. The port which grew up around this new basin was named Port Dundas in honour of Sir Lawrence Dundas, the Governor of the Forth & Clyde Navigation Company. Until the River Clyde was deepened in the mid-19th century, Port Dundas was Glasgow's premier port. In 1825 alone, 98,670 tons of goods were imported into the city along the canal and the famous Swift passenger boats provided regular passenger and parcel services from Glasgow to Edinburgh and all stops in between.

The canal developed into Glasgow's 18th century M8 motorway but instead of *motor* it was boat and the *way* was water – not road. An observer sitting at the side of the busy waterway at that time would have seen many barges and ships sailing past. The barges would in all probability be carrying cargoes of coal and iron while the ships would be delivering wood for the coopers in the local breweries as well as other raw materials necessary to keep the wheels of the new industries in motion.

It goes without saying that the hundreds of barges required to have crews, the many locks needed operators to open and close them and the multitude of other everyday jobs, which were necessary to keep a busy canal operating efficiently, involved the employment of a multitude of *men* – no Equal Opportunities legislation back then!

These thousands of workers were obvious candidates for Christian evangelism and a group of benevolent Glaswegian Christians had a vision to create an organisation which would "... *promote the social, moral and religious welfare of Canal Boatmen ... by the preaching of the Gospel in the Mission Halls, on board boats, and in other places; and the systematic visitation of Canal Boatmen, and other Canal employees, and their families, at home and in their boats."*

Resulting from this, the Canal Boatmen's Institute and Port Dundas Mission was inaugurated in 1870.

A NEW BUILDING

It was decided to construct a purpose-built Institute, in the Port Dundas area of the city, to facilitate the work of the new organisation.

John Keppie, the son of a tobacco importer and a partner with the firm of Honeyman, Keppie and Mackintosh, was appointed as the principal architect for the project and was primarily responsible for the design of the new red sandstone building. However, it is interesting to note that a budding young architect had some visible input in the design and the fine timber roof of the building bore his hallmark. This young architect, who would become one of Glasgow's most famous sons, was born on 7 June 1868 in Parson Street, a stone's throw from the M8 Townhead Interchange which comfortably competes with Birmingham's Spaghetti Junction for Britain's *Most Complicated Motorway Award*. His name was Charles Rennie Mackintosh and, as the world now knows, he would not only become famous in relation to his architectural skills but would also become a household name in relation to his exclusive design styles and art nouveau. The building, which cost £3,000, included a large hall seating 274 and a variety of smaller rooms. The address was 162 Port Dundas Road, Glasgow C.4.

Over the years, both the capital and revenue expenses of the Institute were greatly bolstered by some famous benefactors who, because of their success in the commercial life of Glasgow, wanted to invest something back into the Spiritual life of the city. The list of such people included Lord Bilsland – the bakery tycoon, Sir John Cargill – the oil magnate, Leonard Gow – of shipbuilding fame and Professor Henry Drummond – the Stirling-born scientist and preacher.

One of the perennial problems of city churches is the fact that they do not have the luxury of stable congregations like their countryside cousins. Workers and students can visit a city on an assignment or course of study and, when these are completed, they move on. The declining numbers syndrome arose in the C.B.I. but not for the reasons mentioned above; the use of waterways was declining and the area around the Institute was firmly in Glasgow's plans for future redevelopment. As a result, families were being re-housed in the huge sprawling residential complexes that were fast appearing all over the periphery of the city and, as the people decanted, the congregation declined. In spite of this, the work of the Mission went on unabated.

THE SUPERINTENDENTS

Mr Gilbert

I found it impossible to find anyone who could provide me with first-hand knowledge of the first Superintendent, Mr Gilbert – in fact I don't even know his forename! I found one record that stated he was in charge of the Institute in 1895 during a visit by Henry Drummond. The only other information I could glean was from one of Mr Gilbert's successors – John Houston. In his testimony, he records :

> I was no stranger to the Institute, for as a child I was taken to the Institute by my mother, in the days when Mr Gilbert was Superintendent of the Institute. I still have memories of that old venerable Christian gentleman, and thank God for every remembrance of him.

How important to leave good memories – even to young nippers!

Walter Millar

Mr Gilbert was succeeded by Walter Millar who served the Lord in the Port Dundas Road Institute for a number of years. He moved to the Bethany Hall in Bridgeton in 1925.

William B. Munro

William Munro was in post from 1925 to 1942 and he had an interesting testimony. In the spring of 1903, the resident minister of the church he attended took ill and a substitute minister, Rev. George Johnstone, took the service that day. Mr Munro said that the preacher had *half of Heaven in his face and the whole of Heaven in his message*. After the service, he went for a walk in the city and, in the middle of Dalmarnock Bridge, vowed that he would be a Christian. However, it was not till 8th November, while returning from a walk to Mount Vernon, that he entered Carmyle station in Mount Vernon and committed his life to Christ.
He left his business and joined the Lanarkshire Christian Union and, after helping in the first world-war effort, re-

joined the L.C.U. He then came to the Canal Boatmen's Institute as superintendent but sadly, after 18 years in this ministry, failing health forced him to resign from active work. He went to be with the Lord on 2nd October 1943 and a Service of Remembrance was held for him in the Institute 8 days later.

John M. Houston

In his testimony, Mr Houston says that the Kent Road – St Vincent Church of Scotland will always be a place of happy memory for him because that it was there that the Light first dawned on his spirit and his night was turned to day. For some time after that, he attended Lyon Street Church of Scotland and came under the influence of Godly men who mentored him in his early Christian life. He became a helper in the work at the Grove Street Institute and under the wing of Superintendent George Hood he received much help and encouragement.

He always had a desire to go to Africa as a missionary and applied to the *Regions Beyond Missionary Union*. After John's application was rejected, he received a letter of encouragement from David Findlay, pastor of the Tabernacle. Mr Houston felt that the bottom had fallen out of his world but, within a year, he was invited to become assistant superintendent of the Grove Street Institute. He remained there for 13 years and, after Mr Munro's resignation from the C.B.I., Mr Houston took over the work at Canal Boatmen's in 1943 – in the middle of the second world-war; he remained there till it closed in 1966.

MINISTRY AND ACTIVITIES

The Festive Season

The *162 Port Dundas Road* venue was a hive of activity all through the year but, like most of the missions, they really pulled out all the stops over the Christmas and New Year period. To show the level of activity, the following facsimile shows the schedule of the 1943 – 1944 planned events.

Weekly Activities

While researching some of the historical records for the Institute to get a flavour of their weekly activities, I observed that, at 3.00 p.m. on Sunday afternoons, they advertised a *P.S.A. (for Men and Women)* and, on another document they referred to the *P.S.A.S.* This was a new acronym to me and I had no inkling as to what it was.

Clue number 1 appeared in the 97th Annual Report where, on page 12, we learned that *Henry Drummond was the founder of our P.S.A.* and, in a following paragraph culled from a biography of Professor Drummond, we extracted clue number 2.

Some citizens of Glasgow had founded the Canal Boatmen's Institute in a fine building with a hall, library and club rooms. In the early part of January (1895) the missionary, Mr Gilbert, distributed a large number of circulars calling the men of the district to a preliminary meeting on Sunday, January 20th, at which Professor Drummond and Bailie Bilsland were to be present; and it was intimated that they were prepared, if the movement went on, to give short addresses on subsequent Sunday afternoons. The meeting was full and hearty. A large number of members were enrolled, and the services continued. Good music was provided, and besides pieces from visitors, two or three hymns were sung by the whole gathering.

So now we knew that the P.S.A.S. was founded by Professor Drummond and that it commenced its activities on January 20th 1895 but we still did not know the meaning of the letters of the acronym.

Do we know now? Keep reading!

The Canal Boatmen's Institute had obviously no shortage of events for various age groups and the following list, from the 1964 Annual Report, shows the weekly schedule for that year – including the *elusive* P.S.A. on Sunday afternoon.

®rder of Serbires

Sunday Morning, Foundry Boys' Meeting ... ... at 11 a.m.

Sunday Afternoon, Sunday School ... ... at 1.30 p.m.

Sunday Afternoon, Primary Dept. of Sunday School ... at 1.30 p.m.

Sunday Afternoon, P.S.A. (For Men and Women) ... at 3 p.m.

Sunday Evening, Public Worship ... ... at 7 p.m.

Tuesday, Fellowship Meeting ... . at 7.45 p.m.

Tuesday, Penny Savings Bank ... ... Open from 7 to 8 p.m.

Tuesday, Junior Choir Practice ... ... at 7 p.m.

Thursday, Mothers' Meeting ... . at 3 p.m.

Thursday, Bible Study ... ... at 8 p.m.

Friday, Boys' and Girls' " Glory Hour " ... ... at 7.15 p.m.

Friday, Weekly Prayer Meeting ... ... at 7.15 p.m.

Saturday, Gospel Tea Meeting ... ... at 7 p.m.

THE FINAL REPORT

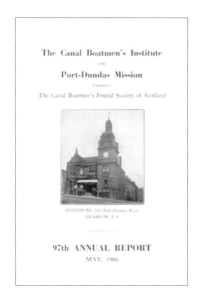

The Canal Boatmen's Institute
AND
Port-Dundas Mission
FORMERLY
The Canal Boatmen's Friend Society of Scotland

INSTITUTE, 162 Port-Dundas Road
GLASGOW, C.4.

97th ANNUAL REPORT
MAY, 1966

Reading through the pages of the 97th Annual Report – the final one – issued in May 1966, two attributes are patently obvious, dedication and faithfulness. Here are three excerpts from the leaders of various departments :

85

Superintendent's Report

Our workers in all departments of the work at C.B.I. have been displaying faith and courage during the past year in spite of the knowledge that soon the work that they have been engaged in at the Mission, for so many years would soon be closing down.

I would take this opportunity to express my grateful thanks to the following ladies who assisted in the running of this meeting for so many years : Mrs Brennan, Mrs Bell, Mrs Crawford, Mrs Elliot, Mrs Gordon and Mrs Probert. May the Lord, Himself, richly reward them for their years of faithful service.

John M. Houston

Sunday School (Primary Department)

It is with a feeling of nostalgia I write this report, knowing it is the last one to be written. Soon the building in which our Sunday School has been held for so many years will be no more, and the association I have had with the School, will be brought to an end.

I became a teacher in 1926 and in the year 1942 was appointed Superintendent of the Primary School. During those years, which have been very happy ones for me, I have been supported by a faithful and dedicated band of teachers, who with me, have told hundreds of boys and girls the wonderful story of Jesus and His love. Eternity alone will reveal the fruit of this labour.

Mr G. McDonald

Sunday School (Beginners' Department)

It is sad to think that this I my last report of my last class in C.B.I. Sunday School. It is with deep regret that we will think of the very building disappearing too.

Personally, I've been in the Sunday School since 1912, first as a scholar and since 1919 as a teacher. I've taught here for 47 years and thought I was going to reach the half century – but that is not to be.

I wish to thank the parents, past and present, for sending their children to learn of God's Word from us. These children, with very few exceptions, were well behaved, scrupulously clean and well groomed in spite of the lack of home amenities, and were indeed a credit to their parents.

We have tried in faith to sow the seed and we leave the increase to God. Only He knows what fruit it may bear to His glory.

Miss Jessie McEwan M.A.

Local children in Wood Street, Cowcaddens in 1910

As I read through the Annual Reports, I not only found the contents challenging but I also felt the emotion and poignancy that the workers expressed for their being involved in the Canal Boatmen's Institute and their faithful dedication to the people of Cowcaddens.

One of the ladies mentioned above in Superintendent John Houston's comments was Mary Elliot and, during the field work for this book, it was my privilege to spend four hours with this dear 90+ year old saint in her 13th floor home in one of East Kilbride's tower blocks. Since my visit, Mary has since gone to be with her Saviour. Mary was known in the Glasgow Mission Hall scene as the *Flannelgraph Wummin*. She showed me notebooks containing handwritten and detailed records of every meeting she had taken over a period of sixty years. She was one of the first people in Scotland to use flannelgraphs as a means of illustrating Bible stories and, although she spoke at all types of gatherings and was the organist in the Boatmen's Mission for many years, she considered that Children's Evangelism was her forte.

In these days of falling away and apostasy, Church leaders would give their right arms to have people of the above calibre in their fellowships but I think it is pretty obvious that, in the *Me, Myself and Mine* society we have created, the odds are stacked against this ever happening - unless, of course, God steps in.

TECHNOLOGY HASTENS THE END

Progress – that's what they euphemistically call it – never stands still. The development of the internal combustion engine, and the frenetic speed of constructing the country's road network, meant that dark clouds of redundancy were hovering ominously over the canal network. Goods could now be moved faster and cheaper by road and the heavy industries were getting lighter as the still-in-progress-today Electronic Revolution kicked in. This meant that, after almost a century of ministry, the raison d'être for the Canal Boatmen's Institute no longer existed.

The 97th, and final, Annual Report of the Mission, dated May 1966, painfully records the following words :

> Today, Port Dundas has ceased to be a port, no boatmen navigate the waters of the canal, and the Mission Hall itself will be demolished in a few months.
> The Directors, therefore, in presenting their ninety-seventh Annual Report, give thanks to God that while the need was there the work was sustained without a break by a continuing flow of dedicated workers. The fruits of their work are treasured memories in the hearts of men and women who, "ransomed, healed, restored, forgiven," give praise and thanks for the new life they found at the Institute.

Modern secular newspapers are not usually known for their kind treatment of matters Evangelical but, in a very faded Scottish Daily Express dated Monday 9 May 1966, in an article by Joseph Mulholland, I found clue number 3 in our search for the meaning of P.S.A.S.

And so ends a dream lasting 96 years

A RED stone building with a clock tower stands on the steeply sloping road that trundles up to the wharves of the old Forth and Clyde Canal.

by JOSEPH MULHOLLAND

visited the poor and the needy and the unfortunate in their houses and in jail when

In his final piece regarding the Canal Boatmen's Institute, the reporter writes :

The canals were teeming too with a hardy race of men – who lived sometimes on the boats they ran and sometimes with their families in Port Dundas. The mission brought to these men – in their homes and on their boats the word of God and the feeling of belonging to a community. The men could listen to talks on the Bible – or they could take tea in the temperate rooms.
Again they could take part in deep and lively discussion in the quaintly named Pleasant Sunday Afternoon Society.

Having found the answer to a clue, Sherlock Holmes used the catch phrase, "Elementary, my dear Watson." With the last four words in the above report, we can say the same because we now know that P.S.A.S. was an acronym for the Pleasant Sunday Afternoon Society. What a lovely name for a church service!

As part of the redevelopment of the Cowcaddens area of the City and the construction of the new northern ring road, the Institute was eventually demolished in 1967. The communion table and chairs were given to a Mission in Greenock and the seat benches were distributed to various missions in the city.

Mr Mulholland concludes his report :

The trustees of the Canal Boatmen's Institute and the Port Dundas Mission can close their Minute Books today knowing that they have done a great job as evangelists and a great one as human beings.

And so say all of us!

Chapter Six

GLASGOW CITY MISSION

If you drive eastwards along the Broomielaw and under the Kingston Bridge, the fourth turning on the left is Brown Street; proceeding up this street will bring you to Crimea Street and, on your left, at the corner, you will see a state-of-the-art building at number 20.

This is the modern Centre of Operations of the Glasgow City Mission; an organisation founded in 1826 but still existing and in vibrant health today.

If you enter www.glasgowcitymission.com into Google you will find another example of this Mission's ability to move with changing seasons and, at the same time, not lose sight of its raison d'être. On the homepage, under an *Everyone Needs Compassion* strapline, the following paragraph appears :

> Glasgow City Mission is the world's first City Mission. Since 1826, we have been showing Christian care to vulnerable adults and children by fighting against poverty and disadvantage in Glasgow.

On their website, there is a 6+ minute video of the various ministries with which they are currently involved and although, over the passing years, their tools and methods have undergone radical changes, it is encouraging to note that their purpose has remained constant.

THE BEGINNINGS

David Nasmith

David Nasmith was born in Glasgow on 21 March 1799 into a fairly prosperous family. At the age of 14, and with two companions, he formed a Bible distribution society. Some years later, he wrote, "This may be marked as the commencement of a new era in my history." Little did he realise, when he penned these words that, during this new era, he would be the means of setting up many institutions which would impact not only his own personal history but also that of a much wider world.

In the early 19th century, there was a national and active interest in foreign missions, typified by David Livingstone the world famous Scottish missionary from Blantyre in Lanarkshire. Apparently, David Nasmith's ambition was also to serve on a foreign field but, for reasons unknown, and historically providential, his application was rejected.
I have in my files a document where it is written that :

> ... it was not until David Nasmith turned his activities nearer home was there any adequate conception of what dark Continents were up the Glasgow closes.

At this time, the population of Glasgow was less than 170,000 but, with the fallout from the Industrial Revolution, it was growing rapidly. While training and working in the manufacturing industry, David Nasmith witnessed the abject poverty and miserable conditions in which some of the city's populace were forced to live. The churches at this time, in line with public opinion, seemed more interested in foreign missions than those at home and it was painfully and patently obvious that something had to be done.

It was back in 1642 that Sir Thomas Browne apparently coined the phrase, *charity begins at home* so it is probable that, by the time David Nasmith was in his late teens, he had come across the phrase. Whether he had or not, we do not know; what we do know is that he took the content of the phrase to heart and, on 1 January 1826, he founded the Glasgow City Mission – a world first for Glasgow!

Before the end of the first year's activities, eight Evangelical denominations had joined the Board of Management and eight city missionaries were working in the field.

THE WORK EXPANDS

Education

The new Mission soon found that putting tracts through letterboxes in the omnipresent tenements, which characterised the streets of Glasgow, was counter-productive for one simple reason – most of the tenants could not read or write. To help solve this problem, evening schools were started in 1827 and scholars were admitted from age 15. The study hours were from 8.00 p.m. to 10.00 p.m. every evening except Saturday.

Police Courts

One of the most important aspects of the Mission's early activities was begun in 1829. This involved having Missionaries in attendance at the Police Courts and, at one time, was officially recognised by them. It is reckoned that this was the forerunner of the modern Probation Service. This service was withdrawn in 1965 after 136 years and the Missionaries relocated to more *normal* duties.

Chimney Sweeps

The Mission also took an active interest in the young boys who were employed as chimney sweeps. The work entailed not only a brush going up a chimney but a boy along with it! These boys were removed from school so early that their education was minimal. Consequently, a school was started exclusively for them in 1831.

Libraries

In the same year, 5 mobile libraries were set up to help the new readers expand their skills. Whether this was accomplished by some sort of horse-drawn carts or manually-drawn carts, we do not know.

... AND EXPANDS FURTHER

As time went on, the Mission acquired some Mission Halls. Some were *shop-front* premises on the ground floor of tenement buildings in the City and others were more *purpose built* for the needs of the Mission.

With such a long history, it is absolutely impossible to document a full chronological record of the Mission's development but it *is* possible to provide a snapshot of their work. How? Firstly, by reference to one of the Mission's Annual Reports and secondly, by interviewing previous Missionaries and people who were regularly found in the various Glasgow City Mission venues.

Let me quote the opening paragraphs of the 1970 Report :

In presenting the 145th Annual Report, the Directors of the Glasgow City Mission give thanks to God for His unfailing goodness during 1970. In the course of its long history, the Mission has faithfully adhered to the principles laid down by its Founders and has laboured incessantly to promote the spiritual and temporal wellbeing of the poorer citizens of Glasgow.

In the first report of 1826, a Missionary was reporting on the fact that a vast number of people had never been taught to read. He wrote, "They know nothing about the Bible, they are without God and without hope in the world. There is no fear of God before their eyes, nor any love to Him in their hearts." That was 144 years ago. Has the situation changed much? In many ways, life has changed since then and almost everyone can read, but there are still many who are without God and without hope in the world. Many who have no fear of God, nor show any love toward Him.

In that first report, after detailing the work of

the Missionaries, the question is asked, "Is there any good likely to be done by all this labour?" The succeeding reports answer that question and for over 140 years The City Mission has been responsible for shedding the light of the Gospel on many darkened souls. Only eternity will reveal how many have yielded their lives to the Lord in a small back street Mission Hall.

THE MISSION HALLS

In the 1970 Report, we read the following :

Since the beginning, The Glasgow City Mission has sought to provide suitable halls in the poorer parts of the City. The Missionary appointed, in addition to other duties, is entirely responsible for all meetings carried out in his hall.

It is a great joy to learn from the reports of the Missionaries that the attendances at our Mission Halls are not only being maintained, but in some cases the numbers are increasing. Work amongst the young people gives much cause for satisfaction. In our Gospel Meetings the Missionary or a speaker faithfully proclaims the Gospel Message, and as a result, men and women are being brought into the Kingdom of God. The Meetings are always bright with singing and musical items from deputations.

This might be a good point to consider the Mission Halls and their ministry to the City of Glasgow.

Coalhill Street, Camlachie

This Mission was situated in the East End of the City just off the Gallowgate and was a thriving work. For a number of years it was led by James Haxton and his nephew recalls being there when the building was packed to capacity. In 1952, at Mr Haxton's memorial service in the Tent Hall, Jock Troup commented that, during his years at Coalhill Street, they had experienced *blessing akin to revival*. He was succeeded at Camlachie by Dan Carmichael who became a well-known figure in the East End. He walked with a very distinctive limp and wore an Anthony Eden hat along with a black coat. He was a Court Missionary.

Open Air in the back courts, Coalhill Street

The 1970 Annual Report mentions that it had been a good year for Coalhill Street Mission :

During the Autumn the Missionary received a letter from a young woman who came to know the Lord at the Mission. She tells of spending the summer on the Continent with "Operation Mobilisation", a Missionary Association working in Europe, and is waiting for the guidance of God for her life of future service for Him. It is very encouraging to hear of converts who are going on steadily for the Lord.
A young married woman, who had drifted away

from the Mission returned and offered her services in the Sunday School. Her help amongst the children has come when needed badly.

Another young married woman came to the Lord in her own home. For some time she has been thinking on spiritual things, feeling that the speakers at the meetings were speaking directly to her. The climax came after she had a vivid dream of a relative – who died a few days later – He asked the question "was she ready to die?" As she felt she was not, this helped her to decide for Christ.

Over the Christmas period, sixty food parcels were distributed. A letter from one couple said that this came when it was most needed.

Crownpoint Road, Calton

This was a shop-front Mission in the Calton district. For a time, this Mission was led by James Brownlee and he was succeeded by David Simpson.

Dervaig Street, Parkhead

This was a corner-shop type of Hall in the Parkhead district. One of the Missionaries who served here was James McVicar. The site has been gobbled up as part of the Parkhead Forge shopping development.

Kintra Street, Govan

This was one of two City Missions in the Govan district and was situated not far from Rangers' Ibrox Stadium. For a time this Mission was led by Harry Martin – a converted communist. The 1970 Report also gives some information regarding this Mission :

The Missionary in his report tells how he helped a mother of four children over financial difficulties. Her husband was unemployed and through lack of knowledge on how to plan her weekly income, she got into serious debt. She owed money to a furniture firm and a warehouse, her electricity and gas were cut off because accounts were not paid.

The Missionary gave her financial help, food tokens and clothing. He then visited the firms concerned and persuaded them to take a smaller amount over a longer period; he also helped her to plan her weekly income. The husband managed to obtain work and she gradually reduced her debt. A neighbour later told the missionary that the woman was so depressed about the debts that she threatened to "put her head in the gas oven and end it all."

One day while visiting in hospital, the Missionary spoke to a young girl of 16 years of age; she was very ill with little hope of recovery. Her young heart was open to receive the Gospel and the Missionary pointed her to the Lord Jesus Christ. She was sent home and the Missionary continued to visit her. Three months later she died and passed into the presence of her Lord

Langlands Road, Govan

This was the second of the two Govan Missions and a Missionary named Billy Smith – apparently quite a *live wire* – served here for a time.

Braid Street, Cowcaddens

This Mission was situated in the north of the City and, again, was a shop-front type of premises. It was originally an independent Mission before the City Mission took it over. Adam Trotter was one of its Missionaries.

Oatlands Mission

This was situated in Logan Street in the Gorbals district. Like the Braid Street Mission, Oatlands Mission started its life as an independent and, for many years was led by David Lamb who was the janitor in the school on the opposite side of Logan Street. It was taken over by the Glasgow City Mission and, for a good number of years, was led by David Boon. David had worked with Jackson the Tailors and, after being approached twice by Adrian Trotter, agreed to become the Missionary.

David Boon, workers and children in Logan Street City Mission

After a time, the Mission relocated to the Church of Scotland Memorial Hall in Pine Street. This was a much more modern building and is one of the City Missions I can remember visiting for the Saturday evening tea meetings, when my wife sang duets with her friend Myra Anderson.

David Boon tells of an event which took place after the move to the Memorial Hall.
One evening, he was in the vestry preparing

for the service when some of the workers came in and informed him that a 'down and out' had come into the hall and that he would have to be asked to leave. David explained that it was for this type of person the City Mission existed. He then asked the workers, "If Jesus were here, would *He* ask him to leave?"
The reaction was apparently instant and silent as, one by one, they quietly left the vestry – lesson learned!

Wyndford, Maryhill Road

This was originally a Brethren Hall which was taken over by the City Mission. For many years the Missionary was Jimmie Wood and he was strongly supported in the work by his own family members. The 1970 Annual Report informs us that :

The extension referred to in last year's report is now complete and proving beneficial to the Missionary. It is being used by the children at Sunday School, Band of Hope and also by a group of forty teenagers who meet on a Wednesday night. On this night, there are games and other activities and the evening closes with an epilogue. The Missionary reports that a number of conversions have taken place. During the summer a number of boys were taken camping. Unfortunately the weather wasn't very good but they enjoyed themselves. A camp is also a help in getting to know and understand the boys.
There are many poor homes in this area and quite a lot of the Missionary's time is taken up with giving much practical help. At Christmas, over one hundred food parcels were given to those in need and also to a number who are housebound.
The Missionary at Wyndford continues to visit some of the stances and talk to the taxi

> drivers. Conversation must needs be short
> between hires. The drivers know that the
> Missionary is available when required if any
> personal matters arise.

There were four halls outside the Glasgow City boundary which were established and funded by Lady Blythswood of shipping company fame. After her death, the City Mission took them under their wing and installed Missionaries to head up the various works.

Douglas Place, Uddingston

I have personal recollections of being in this hall because my father used to go there to speak at the Gospel Meetings and I used to accompany him. The Mission was located in Bothwell Park, just east of Tannochside, and the area now houses an industrial estate. The hall was situated among traditional miners' rows and was a very appropriate location because, like many other evangelical venues at that time, it was heated by a large coal fired stove right in the centre of the hall. For a number of years, James Brownlee, who was previously at the Crownpoint Road Mission, led the work. The 1970 Annual report tells us that :

> The Missionary is very fortunate in that he has a very enthusiastic group of young people. During the summer they visited over 600 homes in the area.
> At the beginning of the year a Gospel Cafe was started and many young people in the area attended. As yet there have been no decisions, but some have shown an interest in the things pertaining to the Christian life. It is the prayer of the Missionary that the Lord will have the victory in their lives.
> At Christmas, a social was provided for the disabled people of the area. A bus collected forty six of them and, after an enjoyable evening, took them home again.

Easton Place, Coatbridge

This was another *stove in the middle of the hall* building and was situated in the Whifflet area of Coatbridge. One of the Missionaries was David Fraser. The 1970 Report makes very encouraging reading regarding this Mission :

During the early part of the year, two Billy Graham films were shown. The attendance at both these films was very good After one of them, two women responded to the appeal and accepted the Lord as their Saviour and have attended most of the meetings each week. Once again, a campaign was held during the summer by students of the W.E.C. Missionary Training College. During this time, every house in the surrounding area was visited and it was found that many were indifferent to the Gospel. One young couple came twice in the last week of the campaign. They have never had any interest in the things of God. Another man contacted is an alcoholic. He came to the meeting one evening and, although under the influence of drink, he sat very quiet. A few nights later he came again, this time he came early and had a talk with the students. After much talking and explaining the things of God, he emptied a half bottle of whisky down the drain. How we pray that, as these people come to the Mission, God's love will break through.

FINAL THOUGHT

I suppose it is possible that David Nasmith was no different from the rest of us in that he was probably very disappointed that his dream of working in a foreign mission field did not come to pass. Who knows?

However, with the benefit of hindsight we are able to see that God had a bigger plan for his life. All over the world there are rescue missions whose formation and continued existence can be traced back to a man from the City of Glasgow – David Nasmith. In the 1830s, he travelled the world and encouraged church leaders to form City Missions and almost 150 pioneer organisations were the outcome. Sadly, not all of them still exist today, but many do and probably the flagship of them all is the London City Mission which was founded in May 1835.

Some men, who spent some of their life as missionaries of Glasgow City Mission, went on to do great work for the Lord in far-flung centres of the globe. Among them are :

John G. Paton – New Hebrides, South Pacific
James Chalmers – New Guinea, East of Malaya
Robert Laws – Livingstonia Mission, Nyasaland (now Malawi)
James Luke – Calabar, West Africa

Although David Nasmith died on Christmas Day 1839, at the age of 39, his legacy lives on today. His life span was short but he was able to pack a lot of urgency into it.

The old Sankey hymn encourages us to do the same :

Haste while the day-beams linger
Haste, ere the shadows fall
Tell them the feast is ready
Tell them there's room for all

Chapter Seven

GLASGOW FOUNDRY BOYS

There is something charming and romantic about cities which have a river flowing through them and names like London, Paris and Rome spring to mind immediately. But Glasgow is also a member of this elite club with its River Clyde. As well as providing picturesque benefits in its upper and middle reaches, the river also provided industrial benefits in its lower reaches as it meandered westward and became *Doon the Watter.*

Its north and south banks housed huge complexes bearing the names of the greatest ship-building yards in the world and earning the coveted brand - *Clyde Built*. These yards used mega tonnes of iron and steel every year and hence there was a marriage of convenience in the city between the river-based industries and the non-river-based industries; between the shipyards and the foundries who supplied the metals required for construction.

A large number of these foundries sprang up in the north of the city in Maryhill and Possilpark near the Forth and Clyde Canal. There was no Health and Safety Executive in those days and consequently young boys of ten, eleven and twelve were engaged to help the skilled tradesmen in their dangerous work and in their even more dangerous workplace. These young boys were not contractually employed by the foundries but were engaged as assistants by the moulders and engineers. Since school attendance was not compulsory, very few of these underage striplings were skilled in any of the *three R's*.

It is impossible to visualise the working conditions that were prevalent at this time – the long hours, the incessant heat from the furnaces, the accident rate, the grime – and, as if all this wasn't enough, the fact that these youths had been thrust into an environment that was anything but a paragon of morality and social graces. They would be subjected daily to a barrage of profanity from life-hardened moulders who would show no deference to their tender ages and minds. Kind begets kind and it is therefore no surprise to learn that many of these young boys turned into the *yobs* and *hoodies* of their day and provided Glasgow with some of its anti-social behavioural problems in the 19th century. A very wise man once said, "there is nothing new under the sun."

THE FORMATION OF THE SOCIETY

In the decade before the Society was formed, an evangelistic effort was taking place in the Cowcaddens and Port Dundas areas of the city under a young man called J. Wakefield MacGill; he was from the Barony Church in Castle Street, Townhead – a church which dates back to the days of Scotland's Covenanter history. In 1855, he started a class for the factory girls who worked in the mills and for the lads who worked in the foundries. Because of the domestic conditions prevalent in the area at the time, Mr MacGill described his target audience as the *gutter babies* of Cowcaddens – maybe not a politically correct definition in today's society but, no doubt, a very accurate one at the time.

In the course of his ministry, he was made aware that a factory girl called Mary-Ann Clough was involved in a work similar to his. Let me quote from a document published in 1965 - the Centenary year of the Glasgow Foundry Boys' Religious Society :

Mary Ann Clough

The first effective Christian work among these boys was undertaken by a young Christian woman, Mary Ann Clough; she was a factory worker who obtained the use of a room in the factory in which she was employed and held meetings on Sunday afternoons, inviting them along to hear what Christianity was about.
She later emigrated to New Zealand and it seemed as if her work had gone for nothing until four young men, Alexander MacKeith, William Martin, William Hunter and James Hunter, inspired by the needs of these lads decided to follow up Miss Clough's work and made plans to establish a Society that would

take an interest in the welfare of the foundry boys, give them opportunities to read and write, and provide healthy occupation for their leisure hours.

This was commenced on 21 November 1865 and was known as :
THE GLASGOW FOUNDRY BOYS'
RELIGIOUS SOCIETY.

THE FOUNDERS

To give a brief profile of the four founders of the Society, the following details have been condensed from articles written by J. Nairn Marshall, a past President of the Society, who had a personal acquaintance with all of them.

William P. Hunter

The first time I saw Mr Hunter was one evening in September 1870 when he came along with Mr Alexander MacKeith as a deputation from the Foundry Boys' Society to the old Cameronian Church in Great Hamilton Street, now London Road. They explained the aims and plans of our Society and endeavoured to obtain a promise that a Branch would be opened in Green Street. Mr Hunter explained the Educational classes, the concerts, entertainments, excursions and the Fair Week trip. Mr MacKeith spoke of the religious side of the work and made special mention of the reasons for having the Sabbath forenoon meeting. The church members and teachers were greatly interested and considered the aims both practicable and desirable. The result was the beginning of the Green Street Institute Branch. Mr David Binnie, an elder, was already a speaker in the Society and helped to smooth over the difficulties of beginning a new sphere of work.

In business, Mr Hunter was a yarn agent and his office was almost exactly where the front door of our present Municipal Buildings is now placed. As with many offices, and even shops in the city at that time, the office was down a few steps from the pavement level with offices above a few steps up thus giving two storeys to which direct access was given from the street level.

In the late seventies he decided to leave for New Zealand and he spent his last Fair Week trip at Lendalfoot. He was just like a boy on holiday and entered into the sports of the lads like one of themselves while, at morning and evening worship, he led the thoughts of all, without any great change of voice or manner, to heavenly things. As a memento of his happy holiday he took with him an album of very amateurish photographs and insisted on paying for it. His whole life was holy and everything he did was consistent with his truly Christian character.

His spiritual power and worth were soon discovered in New Zealand and, shortly after his arrival, he was ordained as Pastor of a congregation. The people were most fortunate to have him and they would be truly led towards a high level of spiritual attainment.

James Hunter

With the name of James Hunter, the first thing that leaps to the writer's memory is the recollection of first acquaintance which also calls to mind a trade of bygone day. When our Foundry Boys' Society was founded, I knew James Hunter slightly in a warehouse where he was a buyer and I was an apprentice. He bought shawls or wraps and his neighbour, Mr Moore, bought Cashmere and *Paisley* shawls.
When the Founders formed themselves into our Society and divided the duties among themselves, James Hunter was appointed Secretary, which office he held for two years. During these two years he was also Superintendent of the Provident Department. Afterwards he became Superintendent of the Social Reform Department.
He was an interesting speaker and in great demand at all the special gatherings of the

Society. He prided himself on being able to secure attention with his first sentence. I can see him yet, when called upon, rising and coming forward, pulling down his linen cuffs and, with a smiling face, state a striking fact. He then, with attractive manner and matter, held everyone interested.

Mr Hunter gave fourteen years of devoted service to our Society and was unstinted in his efforts to promote the interests of the lads and girls. He died somewhat suddenly on 19 May 1879.

William Martin

At the beginning of our Society, Mr William Martin Junior, as he then was, was chosen to be Treasurer and continued to look after our finances nearly all his life. He was an expert in handling figures and we still have the benefit of some of his plans. He always told us, to a decimal point, the average givings of each one attending our forenoon meetings and this little detail still appears in some of our reports. He delighted in details and the Society gained by his care over the little things as well as in the greater financial arrangements.

Mr Martin was no mean executant on the violin and often helped in the concerts of the Springbank Branch, of which he was chairman. A few years later we, in Green Street, enrolled an orchestra to retain the interests of our senior lads. They each paid sixpence a week and were supplied with a violin, a bow and a case, as well as music. These were to be the property of the orchestra for five years when they might be bought by the members at a cheap price. Mr Martin laughed heartily when I told him I had bought the violins by the dozen and he scornfully asked me if I bought them by weight. The orchestra created much interest and increased to about thirty members. Soon other instruments were added. It was not long before Mr Martin began an orchestra in Springbank.

Mr Martin and his sister, who had a lovely contralto voice, were members of the Hillhead Musical Association, which gave popular concerts in the Queens' Rooms in Clifton Street. Mr Martin was not only the chairman of the Springbank Branch but a welcome speaker in all our meetings. He was a strict Sabbatarian. There were in those days no Sabbath buses or tramcars but he never shirked long walks to fulfil engagements at our evangelistic meetings, no matter how far off they might be. I remember him walking round by the Broomielaw Bridge all the way to Govan, again and again. He would not use the ferry although it was available.

Having withdrawn from the Treasureship in his later years, Mr Martin's activities were largely devoted to the interests of his Springbank Branch, of which he remained Chairman till the end in 1905.

Alexander MacKeith

Mr Alexander MacKeith has been called the *Children's Friend*, and he well deserves the name, for no other one, in my experience, in Glasgow, or visiting Glasgow, was more continuous and energetic in the Christ-like effort to bring the young folk under the Saviour's influence than he was. His love for young people, his beautiful mellow voice in speaking and singing, and his simple, natural style of address captivated both old and young. Religion with Mr MacKeith was never a gloomy thing, but a thing of beauty, brightness and joy.

Mr MacKeith was, appropriately, appointed from the very first to be the Superintendent of the Religious Department which was not only most important but one of the most interesting.

While Mr MacKeith gave almost all his time to the work of the Foundry Boys' Society, he from the first took an interest in the *Poor Children's Dinner Table*, and increasingly after the visit of Messrs Moody and Sankey, when the United Evangelistic Association began operations. The first efforts were made from a tent on the Glasgow Green, when at an early hour on Sunday mornings the numerous sleepers lying around on the grass were awakened and invited to a cup of coffee or tea in the Tent. Thus began the Sunday Morning Free Breakfasts.

There is also a monument of which in life he knew nothing, but which stands in the East End of the city. The monument was erected in this way. The Corporation of Glasgow resolved to change the names of streets that were duplicated. There was a Green Street, Calton and a Green Street, Bridgeton. The City Committee thought to change the Green Street, Calton to Tureen Street and to run this name right down from the Gallowgate to London Road and find another name for Green Street, Bridgeton. The Green Street, Calton folk did not like Tureen Street at all and they took means to protest to the Committee against the proposed change. A petition by the bulk of the residents was signed. Armed with this petition a considerable deputation waited on the City fathers, and asked that the name of Green Street, Calton should remain as it is. It was the old path to the Green, it would be better to change the name of Green Street, Bridgeton. It was only a short street and especially there was being built in it a large hall for a Branch of the Glasgow Foundry Boys' Religious Society. The Society had been founded by Alexander MacKeith and others. It was he also who had initiated the Fresh Air Fortnight scheme, and in both of these institutions the East End of the city had fully shared. It was suggested that, in grateful memory, the street might be called MacKeith Street. The deputation left the building, but the Committee agreed to both the suggestions which were to leave the Calton street with its own name Green Street and to adopt MacKeith Street for the Bridgeton street.

So there remains today a reminder of a man who would have been a credit to any street!

IN THE BEGINNING ...

It is not always possible, in researching an organisation's early history - especially a *100 years plus* history – to obtain records of the activities and events which took place during the pioneering days. It is good, therefore, to be able to report that, in the case of this Society, there *are* recorded personal accounts from the pens of the Founders, giving their first hand impressions – warts and all – of the first year's activities and I can do no better than let them speak for themselves.

Religious

Our first Sunday meeting with the boys was held in a dingy, deserted singing saloon, in Cowcaddens, known as the Olympic Hall, which, though very unsuitable, was the best accommodation we could obtain at the time. In the general appearance of the place there was everything to dispel any serious feelings, but the boys seemed in no need of any incitement to noise and misbehaviour. We need not speak of their conduct outside the hall, as that was rather beyond our control; but what it was may be gathered from the fact that a clergyman, who had long successfully conducted a mission in close proximity to our place of meeting, wrote us, threatening to complain to the police of our nightly assembling such a disorderly rabble, and many a time thereafter the police found abundance of work in preserving a reasonable degree of quiet around the place. And then, when the doors were opened, in a style that would have petrified most people, and which even astonished those long used to deal with such rough boys, about 100 of them assembled, more as if some comic piece were to be acted which would be much improved by a little by-play on their part. The clatter of clogs, the promiscuous shouts of "Haw Jock" - "Wull" - "Come 'ere Tam" – then diving under the gallery seats into the vacancy below, and the successful practical jokes thereby possible, made a most appalling beginning. The chairman on the stage, striving to reduce the chaos to order, was more like a captain shouting orders from the gangway in a hurricane; but, eventually, order was obtained, though of a most brittle kind at first. A strange cough, any extra noise from some late comer, a dog barking outside, or such unforeseen circumstances, set our friends up in a moment, either to join in the disturbance or, with mock desire for order, roaring "Pit him oot, pit him oot," "Hear him noo." But, taking advantage of a favourite pause, the chairman has given out a hymn, and all rise up to sing. The hymn-singing had always a most salutary effect, for young people like singing; and when they came to know the words and tunes of the hymns, they did sing.

The opening exercises are short, and adapted to the boys. And now the speaker of the evening comes forward to address the boys. Let him be well prepared, interesting in the extreme, plain and simple; above all, let him present in short and easy words that wondrous story of love, old as the world yet ever new; for he had to deal with an audience who will yield him no conventional attention, or sit still from early trained habit. We rejoice to say, that from the experience of those who addressed these meetings, what was a rude, disorderly rabble at first, sobered down into a still, almost painfully attentive audience.

Education

This part of the Society's operations is one upon which it gives us much pleasure to report. The very regular attendance of most of the boys in their classes, and the decided progress they have made render this branch of our work truly encouraging to all those engaged in it. Generally, the boys on entering the Society are exceedingly ignorant, many ignorant of their letters, and in no case have any been found to have been recently attending any evening classes.

At half-past seven o'clock, on Monday, Tuesday and Wednesday evenings, the school-room doors are opened and the boys, who having only stopped work at six o'clock, have not had too much time to wash off the day's grime and snatch a hasty meal, begin to pour in. Passing the roll-keeper's table, they each call the number which they have on the Society's roll, which is at once noted down and posted into the roll book afterwards. The younger members now take their seats at the writing desks, while the gentlemen in charge issue the copies and pens; the older lads pass into the side-rooms, where reading and spelling are taught on Monday and Tuesday and arithmetic on Wednesday evenings.

At nine o'clock the bell rings, the work is closed with an evening prayer and the boys marched out in orderly ranks.

Provident

The aim of this department is to implant and foster provident habits in the boys, by encouraging them to become depositors in the Savings Bank connected with the Society and in giving them opportunities for expending their

> money economically and beneficially for
> themselves. As the boys pay their weekly
> twopences through this department, and as
> they cannot pass into the Saturday Evening
> Entertainments without going through the bank
> room, this branch of the work is brought before
> them somewhat prominently once a week.
> Every boy is furnished with a Member's Pass-
> book and as this book is also the Bank book
> and has all the particulars of the Cheap
> Schemes printed on the covers, there is little
> danger of forgetting the bank.

AND CONTINUING ...

Looking back, and reading back, it is encouraging to note how the work progressed and grew. Very early in its history girls were admitted to the meetings and in 1886 the Society were able to produce statistics showing that it had a peak membership of 16,560 boys and girls and 1,987 teachers.

When World War I broke out in 1914, numbers declined sharply because many of the teachers and older boys were conscripted into the Forces; this resulted in a slowdown in the development of the organisation.

At the outbreak of World War II in 1939, hundreds of children were evacuated from the city and, again, many of the teachers went into the Forces; some branches closed and never opened again. Also, the population were being relocated to new housing schemes around the periphery of Glasgow and this added to the decline.

However, in the 1965 Centenary Report, the Society were able to declare that they had eighteen branches in the city, from Balornock in the North to Castlemilk in the South and from Cranhill in the East to Drumchapel in the West.

In some ways, the Society resembled the Boy Scouts or the Boys' Brigade because the boys were issued with a uniform and meetings were held in premises not necessarily owned by them. The objective was to provide a Scripture-based knowledge of God and to introduce discipline into the lives of the developing youngsters.

Space does not permit us to detail the various leisure activities which the Society organised and provided but one of them had an interesting sequel.

When the Tsunami which devastated much of Asia in 2004 was over and world-wide appeals were being made for international aid, the Glasgow Foundry Boys' Society responded positively.

The tents which used to be necessary for the annual camps were still in storage but now redundant and the people in the Garngad Branch in Tharsis Street retrieved them and sent them to the disaster area.

The Garngad Branch in Tharsis Street.

A service in Garngad between 1911 and 1926

The Garngad Choir in the "good old days"

The Garngad Band in the same era

120

Chapter Eight

LAMBHILL MISSION

VILLAGE TO SUBURB

Lambhill started its life as a country village less than 10 miles from the foothills of the picturesque Campsie Fells. In the early days of the 20th century, much of the male population spent their work-a-day lives in local foundries, quarries and coal mines; in fact, one of the blackest days in the history of Lambhill was in August 1913 when 22 men lost their lives in the Cadder Colliery disaster.

In 1926, progress decided that Lambhill should become a suburb of the city of Glasgow and within the next decade the sights and sounds of the famous tramcars became part of the local daily scene as they clanged their way to the terminus in Drummond Street (now Strachur Street).

Sadly, on 5 December 1959, the last tram left Lambhill, on route 31, for Merrylee; the end of an era! But another era was in progress.

BEFORE THE MISSION

Back in 1847 the United Presbyterian Church was formed as a result of the amalgamation of the United Secession Church and the Relief Church. During the next half century, other ecclesiastical *re-arrangements* took place within several establishments in the surrounding area until, in 1894, the Lambhill United Presbyterian Mission was formed under the presidency of a gentleman called Robert McLean.

Up to, and through, the turn of the 20th century, the United Presbyterian Mission experienced a time of numerical growth. However, in 1905, some changes were proposed by the church session and the terms were not acceptable to the Mission committee and members; they therefore decided to carry on the mission work on their own and the Lambhill Evangelistic Mission was born.

The picture below shows the original Mission building in 1894; it is the white single storey building abutting the double storey building on the right.

BRICKS AND MORTAR

A piece of ground was acquired in Crawford Street (now Knapdale Street); it soon became a building site and, in due process of time, a new venue was constructed in Lambhill.

December 1906 became an exciting month for it was then possible to plan an opening day; this day arrived on 19 January 1907 when a conference was arranged for the afternoon followed by a social in the evening.

The above picture shows a more recent image of the Church premises.

THE LAMBHILL GOSPEL BAND

During the 20th century decades, I would imagine that almost every evangelical Christian in the west of Scotland had heard of the Lambhill Band – sometimes known as the Lambhill Silver Band – and, like me, had probably assumed that the band was an outreach extension of the Lambhill Mission. Well, we were half correct! Although the members of the Band were also members of the Mission, I discovered during my research that the Band was a separate entity.

In their Jubilee Year publication, titled *Band Testimony*, they explain :

> In writing about the Lambhill Gospel Band, it is necessary to make some reference to the Lambhill Evangelistic Mission and those who founded it. The history of the one is interwoven with the other, and down through the years they have been harmoniously and closely associated, in the spreading of the Gospel.

William Middleton was an early member of the Mission and the founder of the Band; he was born and brought up in Lambhill. In his twenties, he moved to Cambuslang to follow his occupation as a coal miner and while there, he met his wife Jean; he also became a cornet player in the Cambuslang Trades Brass Band.

He was a regular attender of the local Parish Church and, one Sunday, he was arrested by words he read on the flyleaf of a Bible lying on a seat next to him. It said, "Are you a Christian or only a church member?" The question caused him to think but, because of his position as solo cornet player in the Trades Band, he tried to dismiss it; however, in October 1893, he decided to live wholly for Christ. He confirmed his decision at a series of special meetings held by George Clark when the evangelist pointedly asked in his message, "What will *you* do with Jesus which is called Christ?"

After his conversion, Mr Middleton returned to Lambhill and joined with those who were engaged in the Lord's work. The solo cornet player was joined by three other players called Thomas McFarlane, William Crawford and William Millar. These men added a second cornet, a tenor horn and a euphonium to the original cornet thus providing four-part harmony; this is regarded as the beginning of the Lambhill Gospel Band.

Space does not permit to follow the history of the Band but for many long years, in Glasgow and beyond, they were to be heard playing in many missions and to be seen marching in many streets.

The Lambhill Band in 1945

THROUGH THE YEARS

It is always an interesting exercise to indulge in an historical review of life; this can be on a personal level, a national level or, as in our present case, a Mission level. Here are a few items selected from the archival records of the Lambhill Mission.

1927   Tom Rea, an Irish Evangelist held an eight week campaign and over 200 people were converted.

1930   Work started on a building extension in March of this year; it consisted of lengthening the main hall, adding a small hall, kitchen, vestry and two toilets.

1939+   Like most fellowships, many of the members were involved in the war effort, either in His Majesty's Forces or in industries like the coal mining and engineering sectors that required employees to work up extra sweat to support the national war machine.

1940s   This decade records missions and other evangelistic efforts having taken place; the Faith Mission and Seth Sykes are recorded.

1950s   Evangelistic missions again appear during these ten years; names here include Rev. Maynard James, Arthur Campbell, Gordon Voysey, and Rev. Charles Main.

1960s   During the *swinging sixties* evangelism seemed to move up a gear or two at Lambhill with summer Bible classes and children's missions joining the list of organised events. The visiting speaker list was also augmented and included Mrs Bessie Sykes, Rev. Eddie Renton, Jimmy Slater, Rev. Calvin Ritchie (USA) and Rev. O.J. Thomas (London Bible College).
        In 1963, the Mission joined the FIEC but, in 1992, it withdrew its membership on doctrinal grounds.

1975   After some consideration the name of the fellowship was changed from Lambhill Evangelistic Mission to Lambhill Evangelical Church.

From its inception, open air services have been a feature of the Mission along with other events associated with an evangelical fellowship; youth club, Bible class, Sunday school (plus the annual trip!), church choir, etc.

It goes without saying that, of all the attributes which qualified a venue to be considered a Glasgow Mission Hall, a Saturday Night Tea Meeting was paramount and Lambhill followed the example of its sister missions throughout the city. During the winter months deputations would descend on Glasgow G22 from all airts and pairts to sing, play and speak to the gathered congregations with the most important, and expected ingredient of all being present – tea!

GO THEREFORE AND MAKE DISCIPLES

While studying the history of the Lambhill Mission, I was amazed to discover a very interesting statistic; in spite of the fact that the numbers in the Lambhill congregation never reached the levels of its big brother missions in the city centre, it was able to send more than 25 servants into the Lord's work. If that fact was being expressed mathematically, it would say that the large number of people who went into full-time ministry was out of proportion to the number of people in the congregation. That sounds a bit boring and technical but, when we switch the focus from mathematics to geography, it gets quite thrilling to realise that from a relatively small Mission in the north east of Glasgow's urban sprawl, servants of the Lord were sent to Australia, New Zealand, China, India, Ceylon, Africa and some even went as far as Scotland!

THE WORK CONTINUES

A special celebration was held in the Church on 24 February 2007 to mark the centenary of the Mission in Lambhill and a DVD was made of the event.

The work continues today although there are more vacant chairs in the hall than there used to be. However, this is a problem currently shared by many fellowships and assemblies but, after all, the Apostle Paul did warn the Thessalonian saints many years ago that this would happen.

On the positive side, it is encouraging to record that, through the years and in spite of difficulties, the various leaders have stuck to the Mission motto: *Seek ye first the Kingdom of God*.

A MEMORY

The following anecdote is copied from the Band records.

The Stone Thrower

The original instruments of the band were of brass, un-plated, and collected from various sources but the pride of the members in their instruments was only surpassed by their watchful care over them.

One day the band was marching up the road in the direction of Possil when the sound of the music was heard by some boys playing near *the Square*. They ran over and stood on some rising ground near the road known as *The Cutting* to watch the band pass. As it came alongside where the boys were standing, one of them impulsively threw a stone which almost struck the euphonium player. This was too much for the man who thought of the good instrument in his keeping and he ran out of the ranks to get hold of the offender. The young fellow did not wait, however, he was off like a shot and a chase began over the park. The boy twisted and turned in an effort to elude his pursuer but in the end he was cornered and a strong hand seized him. He had obviously immediate expectation of receiving some sharp chastisement but imagine his astonishment when his captor put his hand in his pocket and drew out a copper with the remark, "Here's a penny! dinna' dae that again."

Whatever the band man's intention was to begin with, his wrath must have subsided as the chase proceeded!

Chapter Nine

THE RAILWAY MISSION

In two previous chapters, we have considered ministries that were founded in Glasgow – to evangelise Canal Boatmen and Foundry Boys. We now turn to another industry which employed hundreds of people in the city – the railway.

Unlike the other two industries, the organisation to provide help and support to railway employees was not started in Glasgow; it was founded in 1881 and was called *The Railway Mission.* In its early years, it produced a monthly publication called *The Railway Signal* and I obtained, from the Mission archivist, some pages from the issues dated December 1909 and May 1935; they featured some Scottish news items regarding conferences in Glasgow and Perth. However, what struck me most in reading the articles were the incidences of people coming to faith in Jesus Christ and also the spiritual depth of the subjects addressed by the speakers.

The Mission still exists today but the method of operation has radically changed; it was originally based on evangelisation in mission halls and railway workshops whereas today it operates a chaplaincy service. Its founding objective was *"the moral and spiritual advancement of railway employees of all ages"* and the method by which this had to be achieved was by *"communicating the Christian Gospel to the people working in the railway and associated industries."*

Although the Mission was not headquartered in the city, Glasgow had more branches than anywhere else in Scotland. A List of Branches, published in 1928 by the Railway Mission, shows that, out of a country-wide total of 41 branches, 9 of them were located in the city of Glasgow.

The list records that there were three railway workshops where the Mission was active in evangelistic outreach; they were situated at :

COWLAIRS

Cowlairs is in the Springburn district of Glasgow and a railway depot existed there since 1841. It was the first works in Britain which built locomotives, carriages and wagons in one factory. After passing through two ownership hands, the depot became the property of the London and North Eastern Railway (L.N.E.R.) in 1923 but finally closed in 1968.

HYDE PARK

Also based in Springburn, the North British Locomotive Company was, at one time, the largest locomotive manufacturing company in Europe and the British Empire. As a result of various operational problems, the organisation went into voluntary liquidation in April 1962. The previous Hyde Park site is now the campus of Glasgow Kelvin College.

ST ROLLOX

When the railways were at their zenith, Springburn seems to have been the centre of the universe as far as locomotive construction and maintenance were concerned because the St Rollox works were also situated in the district. Over the years, as the Caledonian Railways and London, Midland and Scottish Railway (L.M.S.) brands disappeared, the original site has shrunk in size to make way for the invasion of Tesco, Costco, Lidl, et al but there is still a railway presence in the form of Knorr-Bresme Rail Services who have one of their five U.K. bases there.

The railway workshops were important in the efforts of the Mission to reach men and women with the Gospel message but more important were the Railway Mission halls; there are more details for some than for others but they were situated in the following districts :

COWLAIRS

A small Mission Hall was situated in Elmvale Road and led by George Allan.

CORKERHILL

Corkerhill is in the Mosspark area of the city, not far from Bellahouston Park. A Railway Village was built there in the 1890s by the Glasgow and South Western Railway Company. It included a Railway Institute which facilitated a range of services for railway employees and their families who lived there. Among the services on offer was a library, a reading room and hot baths. A meeting hall was also part of the complex and the Railway Mission used this facility to hold Sunday Schools, Bible Classes and Gospel Services.

MARYHILL

The work of Maryhill Railway Mission began in February 1896 and, until 1931, services were convened in the Infants' School Room in Main Street. The council decided to demolish the premises and an alternative site had to be found. The temporary site was limited in size and the leaders decided that a more suitable place was required in which the congregation could worship. This was happening during the depression days of the 1930s but, in spite of this, it was decided that they should erect a building. A site was gifted to them and a new building was completed in 1931.

The days of war commenced and, in March 1941, the German Luftwaffe dropped bombs on the area and one of them killed 107 people including many children from the Mission Sunday School. After the war, Mr Sam McIlroy and Mr David Currie headed up the work of the Mission. Railway Missions operated on the understanding that their work was complementary to work carried out by the local area churches. However, after 1945, the work expanded, new outreaches were introduced and a Sunday morning worship service was started. Many of the men got involved in the Scottish Festivals of Male Voice Praise which opened fresh doors of contact and led to new friendships being formed and expanded ministries being set up.

In the early 1970s, it was decided that the Mission building, which had been built in the 1930s, was now past its *sell-by* date and required replacement. Demolition and rebuilding got under way and the new premises were officially opened on 24 October 1971. During the same period, the presence of the railways in Maryhill was diminishing and it was felt that it was an appropriate time to change the name of the Fellowship. Consequently, the old Maryhill Railway Mission rebranded itself and became *Maryhill Evangelical Church* and it is encouraging to report that the work and witness still continues today in Cumlodden Drive.

Maryhill Evangelical Church

POLMADIE

There were large railway workshops in the south side of Glasgow and consequently, the Railway Mission opened a branch in Polmadie Road. Oliver Hodgson was the leader. The premises had previously been a butcher's shop and the congregation could experience quite a *chilling* atmosphere because they were surrounded by floor-to-ceiling and wall-to-wall white tiles!

SHETTLESTON

Shettleston had a small but attractive Railway Mission in Annick Street and the leader was Stanley Boon – the father of David Boon who was a Glasgow City Missionary. Again, *progress* and redevelopment forced the closure of this venue.

TOWNHEAD

The Railway Mission Hall in Tennant Street also disappeared in the M8 redevelopment project at Townhead.

SPRINGBURN

Pastor D.J. Findlay of St George's Cross Tabernacle was involved in the commencement of the Springburn Branch of the Railway Mission. He writes :

More than fifty years ago I rented for a short time a triangular shop at the corner of Vulcan Street and Springburn Road, and in that shop the Mission had its birth.
For a period we, ourselves, conducted a week-night service there, and in those humble surroundings God gave a wonderful season of revival blessing, during which hundreds of men and women were brought to Christ. In that time of revival several of the existing churches in Springburn were born and the Railway Mission was formed to conserve and carry on the good work.

Mr Findlay's facts are confirmed, and others added, in an extract from "The Railway Signal" where the writer uses a much more brusque and imperial style of language than Mr Findlay.

> This Branch was commenced in the year 1887, meeting for a time in a hired hall in Vulcan Street and holding cottage meetings every Tuesday.
> In 1889 the Branch sent a delegate to the Annual Meetings in London and he reported thus :- "Our work started about two years ago. God has blessed us among Railwaymen and others. There is open-air work all the year round, in all weathers. We have no hall of our own but want one badly and mean to get it. We have a large room over a cooking depot, and it is full for the Gospel Services on Sunday. Our kitchen meetings are wonderful. We are under notice and may have to move out at any time. The Company have kindly granted us ground, but we want the money. Remember, there are from three to six thousand Railwaymen around us and we want them saved. Pray for us."

A Jubilee Celebration booklet was published in 1937 to commemorate the Mission's first 25 years and, from it we can learn some more details.

The Celebration booklet contains personal recollections and memories of people who were actively involved in the early days of the Springburn Mission. Names of various people are mentioned, two of whom went to Brazil and Congo as missionaries and others to fields nearer home. For many years, the Mission followed the blueprint of their city peers in scheduling Gospel Services, prayer meetings, Saturday tea meetings and, on a Wednesday, the hall filled with boys and girls for their *"Glory Hour."*

From 1920 – 1926, the work was overseen by John Sim. He pays tribute to Mr William McKinnon, Mr James Macgregor and Mr William Strang whom he considers "great pioneers" in the Springburn story. John Sim graduated to become the Rev. John Sim and became the minister of the Church of Scotland in Duns, in the Scottish border county of Berwickshire.

Following John Sim's term of office, George Scott became the President of the Vulcan Street Mission in 1927 – a post he held for 38 years till, as a result of a heart attack, he went to be with the Lord on the last day of January 1966.

George Scott

During his years of faithful service, many people were born again and many left the Mission to enter full-time service for God; among the names, John Kerrigan to the Baptist Church in Kirkintilloch, John Ramsay to the Church of Scotland in Saltcoats and William Johnstone to active missionary work in Brazil.

George Scott's death was a great loss to the Railway Mission and, at the A.G.M. in May 1966, it was unanimously agreed to ask Bill and Betty Smith to fill the gap – Bill as president and Betty as organist.

Betty Smith was a daughter of Seth Sykes, the Evangelist; their Welcome Social was conducted by Rev. Robert Telfer of Palermo Street Congregational Church at which various people spoke and sang.

Bill and Betty Smith

The organ from the Prayer Room in Vulcan Street Mission.
Still in use today in David and Ada Ward's home in Kilsyth.
(Seth Sykes' grand-daughter)

Under their leadership, the work continued for a number of years and many souls were saved. However, a sad letter arrived from the *Glesca Cooncil* informing the congregation that they had to vacate their hall by March 1982 because the relentless hand of re-development was about to visit Springburn and present it with a new by-pass.

The Springburn By-Pass under construction

A new Baptist Church had recently opened in Springburn and the people from Vulcan Street Railway Mission were invited to attend the services there. Consequently many of them transferred to the new Fellowship to worship and, along with the members, they transferred the Women's Meeting as well!

One of the *regulars* who had attended Vulcan Street was Seth Sykes and it would be remiss not to give some details of this *Great Little Man* as his biography is entitled.

SETH SYKES

Seth Sykes has become one of Glasgow's best known sons and has his own place of honour in *The Glasgow Story* on the world-wide web. He was born on 23 July 1892 in Springburn and was third in a family of five. In his brief biography, he relates his personal testimony :

When I returned home, I ventured near an open-air meeting in Vulcan Street. The song they were singing seemed directed to me by the Spirit of God, as was the invitation to come to the Mission Hall to hear a well-known speaker of those days, Mr Alan Stewart, District Secretary of the Scottish Railway Mission. The last verse of that song helps us to understand how the Lord was speaking directly to me, although I was one of the many standing around.

> Whosoever will, the promise is secure
> Whosoever will, forever shall endure
> Whosoever will, 'tis life for evermore
> Whosoever will may come

Following the workers down to the hall, I listened with interest to the speaker as he told the story of Redeeming Grace. Like John Wesley as he sat in the little chapel in Aldersgate, London, 'I felt my heart strangely warmed.' The result was that I sought the Lord's forgiveness and restoration in the quietness of the little vestry, where one of the workers pointed me again to the Word of God as my only hope to guidance and cheer.

That wonderful day, 8th November 1908 when a poor wandering backslider was restored and forgiven, stands out as the turning point in my life, for, being a lively young man and having strayed already, there is no saying where the Devil might have driven me.

Within one month, and using a shilling (5p today) given to him by his father, Seth paid the membership fee, joined the Railway Mission and was presented with the certificate shown below and bearing his name :

In 1913, Seth became a motorman with the Glasgow Corporation Tramway Department based at the Possilpark Depot but his zeal as an Evangelist was constantly developing. In 1914, he married Jessie Robertson, a worker in the Railway Mission. The same year, after the outbreak of war, Seth joined the army and, after discharge, re-joined the tramway service. During the following years, three girls were born into the Sykes' home and happiness seemed complete. However, the happiness was suddenly shattered through the death of his beloved wife Jessie.

Although lonely, broken-hearted and visibly passing through the valley of the shadow of death, his faith in Jesus was strong as he sought for Divine guidance. At that time, a young lady called Bessie Greer was actively testifying in Word and song throughout the city and, on hearing of Seth's loss, she sent a message of comfort to him. At a later date, they met on a Gospel platform and began to take meetings together. Love developed and they were married on 16 July 1925.

Both of them had previously written Gospel songs and one of the best known choruses in the world was jointly written by them in a railway carriage between Edinburgh and Glasgow. It has been translated into more than 70 languages throughout the globe including French, German, Arabic and Chinese. I'm sure we will hear it one day in a perfect and Celestial environment, being sung by *a multitude that no man can number*. I'm not sure what the language will but I eagerly anticipate the event!

Here is the chorus :

Seth continued to work on the trams during the day and together, with his wife Bessie, conducted meetings at night;

they were sometimes helped by "*the tiny tots trio*" – Betty, Ada and Jessie – his three girls, and lantern lecture slides were used as visual aids. This pattern of lifestyle continued for a number of years but, in 1929, Seth gave up his job in Glasgow and, along with his wife, became full-time evangelists for Christ. In a later brochure, celebrating twenty years of ministry, Seth recorded some details surrounding their decision :

It ALL began through reading a book, *The Life Story of Chas. E. Cowman*, written by his wife. This book was sent to us by our friend, Mr John McIlveen of Lambhill. After reading this book, we prayed and felt that God was definitely calling us out as full-time evangelists.

We were very busy as it was – meetings almost every night, and many friends in our district will remember our open-air work among the children in the meetings held at Alford Street. It scarcely seemed possible that we could do any more. Some days before, Rev. H.A. Stirling, visiting us prayed that "the Lord would enlarge our borders" and truly He thrust forth labourers into His harvest when He called us.

We had many critics who tried to discourage us, some who would have turned us from our purpose because instead of being "zealous of good works" they were "jealous of good works," but, in spite of various difficulties we were determined to obey the call, knowing He was with us

Their first *away* campaign was in a Methodist Church in Derby but doors also opened up in Manchester, London, Belfast, Guernsey and many other places in England and Ireland. They were also kept busy in Scotland with regular visits being made to venues in Edinburgh, Aberdeen and other parts of the country. Many souls were won for Christ by the Lord blessing their ministry. One person, who knew

Mr Sykes as a personal friend said, "Seth was not just a *preacher*, he was also a *reacher*." A fitting compliment!

Their parish also, and obviously, encompassed their own beloved city and the list of places they visited includes many of the venues which are the subjects of this book – The Tent Hall, Bethany Hall, Canal Boatmen's Institute, the Railway Missions and many others.

Their family increased one Christmas Eve by the birth of another "Seth Sykes" and a few years later by the birth of his sister Evangeline.

In 1949, Seth and Bessie celebrated twenty years of full-time ministry in the Lord's work and the occasion was marked by a celebration in the Tent Hall. Let me now quote some paragraphs from his biography :

On the 16th July 1950, they were in the midst of a campaign in the Seamen's Chapel, Brown Street, Glasgow, this having taken the place of the usual seaside services at Largs, cancelled due to unforeseen circumstances.

On that date they celebrated their Silver Wedding, a very happy occasion which was made even more memorable by the friends there who provided a lovely tea, and by the fact that souls were saved that night in the evening service.

They later went to Lisburn C.W.U., Aberdeen and Port Glasgow but the shadows were gathering – "the sands of time were sinking."

Mr Sykes was becoming noticeably thinner and more easily tired and this was a secret anxiety to his wife and friends. He persistently declared that he was all right, however, and so time went on.

Halfway through the campaign at Port Glasgow he took suddenly and seriously ill and, to make a long story short, he was swiftly removed to the Royal Infirmary, Glasgow. An immediate operation for a perforated duodenal ulcer was then performed and despite much united prayer on his behalf he passed away a few days later on the 29th November 1950.

He had asked his wife to carry on the work if he should be called home and, up to the last, his thoughts were for her and his family.

The photograph below was taken in 1949 and is the last one of the family together.

Charles Wesley once said, *"God buries His workmen but carries on His work."* This was certainly the case after Seth Sykes had run his earthly race because, as he had requested, the baton was picked up by his wife and the work carried on, in spite of the fact that her children were aged eleven and six respectively.

Mrs Sykes was born, as Bessie Brown Greer, into a Baptist family, on 21 March 1905 in the Calton district of Glasgow. In her early life, musical skills were becoming obvious and, two years after receiving the Saviour into her life at the age of fourteen, she had written a number of hymns including – "Listening In", "Evermore the Same" and "Just Like the Saints of Old."

Her spiritual growth in Hermon Baptist Church, in Cathcart Road, was under the ministry of Rev. Duncan McNeill and other men of God. As she developed, her abilities became known throughout Glasgow and farther afield and she was in great demand for speaking and singing at meetings.

Bessie Sykes had a unique style and depth of ministry and, after her husband's death, it deepened even more. Two of the hymns she wrote around that time probably reflected her inner emotions with the titles, "Go and Tell It All to Jesus" and "All the Way to Glory." She also composed the music to "You'll Never Be Lonely" – the lyrics had been previously written by an old man in Dublin.

In 1979, Mrs Sykes celebrated 50 years of faithful service for the Lord and, in a leaflet printed to honour the occasion, there is an interesting paragraph – let me quote it :

> Possibly Mrs Sykes' greatest gift, as reliable today as ever, is her memory. Without using words or music, whether using hymns of her own choice or chosen by others, more modern or going back many years, unfalteringly there emerges a few notes of music in that lower register and she SINGS; verses and choruses of anything chosen. She has never been known to pause to think, never to waver for one moment and one wonders just how many hymns she knows and can recall at will.

As Christians, we are commanded not to *covet* anything but I must admit to a twinge of jealousy while reading the above words!

Bessie Sykes went to be with her Saviour on 29 July 1982, at the age of 77 and her body was laid to rest, beside her husband in Lambhill Cemetery in the north of her beloved city.

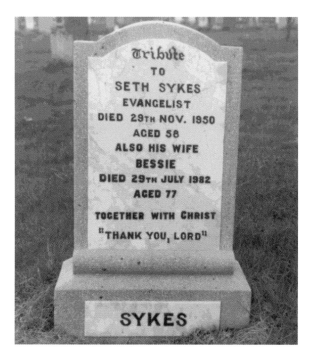

I have taken a final, and suitable, epitaph from Bessie's 1979 Jubilee Praise publication :

Countless people are indebted to the ministry of Seth and Bessie Sykes. Some are already in the glory and others on their way to it, while yet others are found in various types of Christian ministry.

Chapter Ten

THE TABERNACLE

WHEN IS A MISSION HALL NOT A MISSION HALL?

I was in two minds as to whether to include this chapter in a book about the Mission Halls of Glasgow because, if we are nit-picky and strict with our definition, the final product, which evolved as St George's Cross Tabernacle, was *not* a Mission Hall. And yet, on its journey to get there, it did pass through recognisable phases which made it *look like* a Mission Hall. Also, its history dates back to the Moody and Sankey era when some of the other Mission Halls came into existence in Glasgow and many names that feature in the historical records of the other Halls are found in the archives of the Tabernacle. These include James Scott and Lord Maclay and the G.U.E.A. also features in its early days.

The most obvious and striking difference between the Mission Halls and the Tabernacle was the style of leadership. The government of the Missions included a certain amount of democracy while the Tabernacle, for over half a century, was governed by one individual – David J. Findlay.

In his biography of Pastor Findlay, published in 1949, Alexander Gammie includes the following paragraph :

> He carried himself with such an apparent weight of authority that it seemed natural for him to be dominating and masterful. His life-long friend, Dr Duncan Main, of Hangchow, once said in his own witty way that he had 'never known Pastor Findlay play second fiddle, but he had never known him blow his own trumpet.' He was as autocratic in some of his ways as General Booth and he had other qualities in common with the founder of the Salvation Army. And he ruled his congregation in the Tabernacle as Dr Parker ruled his in the London City Temple. He was not only its Pastor, but also its treasurer and its deacons. No one questioned his rule or dared to challenge his decisions. He was the personification of a spiritual dictator.

I have included this point as an observation and a comparison but not a criticism because, as we view our world today, including our own islands, democracy cannot be hailed as a wonderful paragon or an ideal style of government.

David J. Findlay attended a meeting in the Wellington Street U.P. Church where Dr Alexander Maclaren, of Manchester presented the simple Gospel message. Following that service, a meeting was conducted by D.L. Moody on the other side of the street in Ewing Place Congregational Church and, at that service, on 3 March 1874, David Findlay accepted God's offer of personal salvation.

THE BEGINNINGS

Pastor David J. Findlay

It became apparent, in the months following his conversion, that the young Findlay was destined for the pulpit. In the autumn of 1874 he was asked to speak at a house meeting in Townhead where about 20 people regularly gathered in Stanhope Street. Sometime later, along with two friends, he launched a Kitchen Meeting in the home of a Mr and Mrs Hughes at 19 Church Place in the Garscube district of the city. This project regularly attracted up to 50 people and continued for about 2 years.

With growing numbers, a larger venue became a priority and, in the autumn of 1876, the G.U.E.A. opened a new building at 2 Possil Road and the *Kitchen Meetingers* were granted use of the premises. Unfortunately, this lease only lasted for one year but, during that year, the congregation often comprised 300 people.

The house in Church Place (middle floor – small x next to window)

From November 1877 the work continued for the next 4 years under the G.U.E.A. flag and the nomadic congregation were offered the use of a hall in Grove Street by a Mr J. Wakefield MacGill – but only on a Sunday. The years in Grove Street were among the most fruitful in the history of the group's development and records confirm that many people came to Christ – sometimes up to 50+ on one night.

The next flit was to the Windsor Hall in Great Western Road where they continued for 2 years. Again, only Sunday services were possible here and, for week-night services, halls were rented in Seamore Street, Kelvin Street and elsewhere in the district.

In 1884, a new hall was erected at 243 Garscube Road in the heart of their original district. It was meant to be a *Penny Theatre* but the Lord had other plans. When the builder completed the contract, he knelt down among the bricks and mortar and prayed that the place would never be used as a theatre but asked God to send someone there to preach the Gospel. Mr Findlay was that *someone* and he later commented that the builder's petition was certainly not to be counted in the list of *unanswered prayers*.

Garscube Hall became the hub of the work for the next decade. This was a period where the Mission Hall definition certainly did apply because the Hall was situated among some of the worst slums in Glasgow and drunkenness, prostitution and crime were the next door neighbours. In spite of this (and maybe because of it!), hundreds of souls were saved during the years in Garscube Hall.

ANOTHER GLASGOW TENT

In a previous chapter of the book, we featured a tent that the folk east of city centre had used on Glasgow Green. Not to be outdone, the folk west of city centre did the same. The history in the paragraphs above spans the twenty year period from 1874 – 1894 and, in all of those years apart from the first, a summer-long tent mission took place from the end of May till the end of September. Pastor Findlay records that these 18 week-long missions were fatiguing but were also most fruitful for the Kingdom of God.

Group of Tent Workers at St George's Cross in 1885

The tent was pitched east of the site that eventually housed the Tabernacle. The later tents were able to seat 1,000 hearers but frequently the sides had to be let down for an overflow congregation outside.

THE ANNUAL CONFERENCE

An event, which in later years became a feature of the Tabernacle ministry, had its origins in the tent namely the Annual Conference usually held during the last week of September. Among the list of speakers at the first Conference in 1880 we find the name W. J. Govan, the founder of the Faith Mission.

THE TABERNACLE

The Tabernacle was built in 1894 and the first meeting held in it was the Annual Conference at the end of September that year. Who could better know the events leading up to the construction of the building than Pastor Findlay. Let me quote from his pen in 1924 :

Pastor Findlay in his vestry in the Tabernacle

For many years every eligible building site within a radius of half a mile or more had been taken up, and many wondered why that particular piece of ground was kept free for our Tent Missions each summer. There were legal difficulties in the way of the purchase of the land, but to us there was another and more satisfying reason. We ourselves, and others, had been led for years to pray that the ground might be kept for the preaching of the Gospel, and that upon it a permanent building should be erected to house the work. At length, when the time for action seemed to have arrived, the first thing we did was to try to attain an answer to our prayers by stepping out of the path of simple faith and waiting upon God. We approached a wealthy Christian man with whom we were slightly acquainted, and laid our desires and plans before him. This gentleman at once entered into the plan with great enthusiasm, and promised to provide all the money that was needed to complete the project. It is not necessary to tell the whole story in detail here; suffice it to say that various legal difficulties sprang up in connection with the title to the ground, and rights of neighbouring proprietors, which necessitated a long process in the Law Courts in Edinburgh. By the time this was completed, and the ground came to be offered for sale, our wealthy friend had apparently changed his mind, or at all events he failed to implement his promise. He never explained the matter to us, and we did not ask him to do so, having by that time become aware of the mistake we had made, and being deeply thankful to the Lord for delivering us from the result of our error. The coveted piece of land became the property of a well-known builder in the city, and he proved to be – all unknown to himself – the instrument God had chosen to build a house for Himself at St George's Cross; and so the first Tabernacle was built and we entered on occupancy under a lease which – repeatedly renewed – remains operative to the present time. The main auditorium had accommodation for about 1000 persons, and there was a side hall and several other rooms. After twelve years, the first building began to prove inadequate for the growing work, and then by the generosity of some of our friends we were able to take it down and reconstruct it in its present form. Now the main auditorium has seats for 1400, and we have a useful suite of twelve smaller halls and rooms, which together form a beehive for all sorts of spiritual energies which may be rightly connected with the Kingdom of God.

The platform at the re-opening service on 12 December 1907

Part of the audience at the re-opening service on 12 December 1907

As we review the history of the Church in the last half century and consider some of the *bait* that has been used to attract new *fish* into the Gospel net, maybe even in some of the Fellowships many of us have attended, it can often make us blush. Also, as we view the contents of some of the programmes which the satellites now stream into our living rooms and the continual soliciting for more funds which accompany many of them, it begs the question, "Was this what Jesus meant when He said, 'I will build My Church'". I think not!

Let me quote again from Pastor Findlay regarding the principles he used in the governance of St George's Cross Tabernacle :

It may be well to state here in a few words the principles on which the work has been carried on from the beginning, and from which we have never seen any reason to deviate. We unhesitatingly accept the whole Bible as the fully inspired Word of God, and find and have always found in it alone all that we need for life, Godliness and ministry. We have never ourselves taught – nor have we ever called to

> our help men who teach – anything that contradicts the old-fashioned Evangelical doctrines which have proved the Power of God unto Salvation through all the ages. We have always endeavoured to proceed on spiritual lines, and have never introduced – nor had any temptation to introduce – anything of the nature of "entertainment." Our income in recent years was usually between two and three thousand pounds, and this large sum comes in almost entirely through the freewill offering boxes at the doors; we never make any personal appeals for money and never "take up collections." We have always taught our people that "the Tithe" is the foundation unit of Christian giving, and that systematic freewill giving to the Lord brings big blessings into the hearts and lives of His people. More than half of all our income goes towards the support of our Missionaries.

Makes you think, doesn't it?

THE WEEKLY SCHEDULE

In keeping with other Evangelical Missions in Glasgow, the Tabernacle had a busy schedule of weekly activities. Here is a list of the regular services taken from the biography of Pastor Findlay written by Alexander Gammie and, in keeping with the other Missions, notice the pre-eminence given to prayer.

Lord's Day

10.00 a.m.   Missionary Prayer Meeting
11.30 a.m.   Christian's Service
12.30 p.m.   Lord's Supper (on first Lord's Day of month)
2.00 p.m.   Prayer Meeting
2.30 p.m.   Young People's Meeting
5.00 p.m.   Sabbath School
5.00 p.m.   Young Women's Bible Class
5.00 p.m.   Young Men's Bible Class

5.45 p.m.	Prayer Meeting
7.00 p.m.	Evangelistic Service

Tuesday

7.15 p.m.	Prayer Meeting
8.00 p.m.	Evangelistic Service

Wednesday

3.00 p.m.	Mid-week Service
7.00 p.m.	Junior Y.P.S.C.E.
8.00 p.m.	Senior Y.P.S.C.E.

Thursday

7.30 p.m.	Prayer Meeting
8.00 p.m.	Fellowship Meeting

Friday

7.00 p.m.	General Prayer Meeting

When we study this list, it is hardly surprising that, during these bygone days, many lost souls were won into the Kingdom although it may be more correct to say that they were *prayed* into the Kingdom. Oh that we could see these days again and I suppose we could, if we were willing to pay the same sacrificial price that our forefathers did.

... AND MRS D.J. FINDLAY

In presenting a brief overview of the St George's Cross Tabernacle and the sterling work done by Pastor David J. Findlay, it would be remiss if we did not mention the fact that, behind the man, there was a lady.

Mr Findlay had been a member of Adelaide Place Baptist Church. One of the deacons in the fellowship was vacating one of his shoe retail business premises at 255 Argyle Street and D.J. Findlay took it over. The deacon in question was a Mr William Quarrier and the reason for his leaving the business was that he felt it necessary to devote his whole time to a rapidly expanding work for destitute children. The clue is in the name and this work was, of course, the Orphan Homes of Scotland in Bridge of Weir which eventually housed up to 1,500 children at a time. This was not to be the last link between the names Findlay and

157

Quarrier for, on 12 December 1882, Pastor Findlay married Isabella Elgin Quarrier, the eldest daughter of Mr and Mrs Quarrier.

He later testified that the greatest possible blessing – next to Salvation – came into his life that day and he admitted that the work owed much more to her than it did to her husband.

After further decades of faithful ministry, Pastor Findlay took charge of the services in the Tabernacle on 12 June 1938 not realizing that this would be the last visit he would make to his beloved sanctuary. Two days later, shortly after noon he took a heart attack and died, five days before his eightieth birthday. Mrs Findlay survived her husband by almost seven years. She died on 18 May 1945 in her eighty-eighth year. Both are buried in the cemetery of the Orphan Homes at Bridge of Weir.

... NOT FORGETTING THE FMVP

It would be remiss if we omitted to mention the fact that the St George's Cross Tabernacle has another claim to fame in that the Festivals of Male Voice Praise movement had its origins there.

The Tabernacle Choir was founded in 1891 and continued for about four decades. However, by the winter of 1928/29, membership had reached an all-time low with only two men remaining – James McRoberts and George Freckleton. They met to pray and, rising from their knees, George said to James, "If you become leader, I'll become secretary" and so Mr McRoberts became director of the Tabernacle Choir. Their prayers were positively answered and numbers soon increased to sixteen and opportunities for witness opened up.

A Male Voice Festival in the Tabernacle with James McRoberts directing the Choir and James Fitch at the piano

By 1934, some choirs had formed in Glasgow and were fulfilling engagements in the city churches and mission halls. Male voice choirs were also being formed in other areas of Scotland and Northern Ireland. James McRoberts felt led of the Lord to call together the leaders of several choirs in the West of Scotland to consider the possibility of amalgamating the choirs in a visible and united testimony. The objective was: to form a massed chorus for a Festival of Male Voice Praise (FMVP) and a speaker would be invited to give a closing Gospel message.

The first such Festival was held in the Tabernacle in 1935 on Saturday 4th March. Pastor D.J. Findlay chaired the event, Lindsay Glegg from London was the speaker and the choir was a combination of five local choirs.

Several areas in Scotland were now holding their own local festivals and, in 1944, the Glasgow, Renfrew and Lanark district choirs combined and, with a chorus of 300 voices, the first *All Scotland Festival* was held in St Andrew's Halls at Charing Cross.

THE WORK CONTINUES TODAY

It is encouraging to report that, unlike many of the Mission Halls featured in this book, the work still continues today.

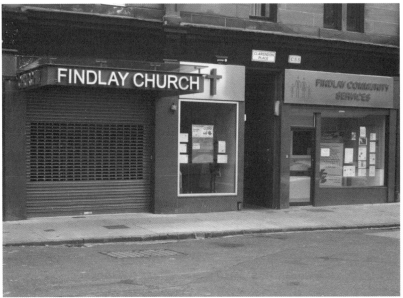

The unobtrusive shop fronts conceal the Gospel work behind them

It went through a process of re-branding and is now simply known as Findlay Church. A visit to their website (www.findlaychurch.co.uk) reveals an active centre of Evangelism; their vision statement is *To Make God's Love Visible* – and they do!

Chapter Eleven

OTHER MISSIONS

As well as the Missions detailed in the previous chapters, the city of Glasgow could boast of many smaller missions and fellowships scattered throughout the metropolis. Sadly, not too much archival documentation seems to have been produced and this chapter is an attempt to record as many facts as possible, culled from human memories as well as any available sources.

Two consequences of following this course of action is that firstly, we have less information to print for every mission and secondly, there is the possibility – maybe even the probability – that a mission is forgotten and not included. If this has happened, can I ask for your understanding in advance? Although there may be less data shown against these *Other* Missions, this in no way implies that their evangelistic effort and outreach was of less importance than their big brother Missions in the city because, at the end of the way, and the end of the day, it is *faithfulness* that is God's criterion for evaluation, not size and numbers.

The Missions are listed in alphabetical order.

ARTIZAN'S HALL

This was in Teviot Street in the Kelvinhaugh area of the city. One man associated with this mission was Alex Morrison; he was a fine Christian man who had a great understanding of the Scriptures having read through the Bible about 60 times. He worked with the Post Office and was apparently a great encourager of others – a real Barnabas!

Two other people involved in this work were John White and Alex Cordiner. John White later went to the Tolbooth Mission.

The hall was closed in July 1971, Mrs Mary Elliot being the closing speaker.

BARDOWIE STREET GOSPEL MISSION

The roots of this Mission go back to 1878 when a young man called John Allan began kitchen meetings in his mother's home in Barloch Street. He then rented a shop in Bardowie Street and a Gospel Mission was formed. In 1892, John Allan and a group of Christian workers leased a piece of ground from Fairfield Laundry and built a hall. The venue was opened in June 1893 and was named Bardowie Street Mission Hall (Allan's Mission to the locals!) For 36 years the Gospel witness went from here but, in February 1928, notice was served by the Council to say that they had purchased the ground for house building and that the hall was to be demolished. A letter was written to the authorities requesting other ground be made available in the area to rebuild. The result was that the ground on which the present hall stands was given on lease and the building work was carried out; the opening ceremony took place on Saturday 18 October 1930 and the official name of the hall would now be known as Bardowie Street Gospel Mission. It is encouraging to report that this work continues today in Possilpark.

BRIDGETON EVANGELISTIC MISSION

To the locals, this venue was better known as "Donnelly's." It was entered firstly through a "pen" – an opening between the tenement buildings – and then up a wooden stair to a small hall above a rag store. In today's bureaucratic red-tape world, it would not have passed the first word of the first sentence of the first paragraph of the statutory regulations!

There was little ventilation and, when the proverbial Glasgow Mission tea was being brewed, it added to the sauna-like environment. The meetings were always packed to capacity and, a person who was around at the time referred to it as a "flea for all."

On the positive side, it appealed to many of the poorer folks in the area and they attended night after night after night. The leader was Willie Donnelly and he was assisted by a younger man named Walter Rossendale.

CARRICK STREET

This was a lodging house Mission just off Broomielaw, an area like so many others in Glasgow, which, for years has been in the hands of redevelopers. It was an outreach work from Finnieston Church of Scotland and Dr D.M. McIntyre, the principal of the Bible Training Institute in Bothwell Street, used it to give practical experience to his students.

CARTER'S MISSIONS

We rank our delivery vehicles today by the horsepower of their engines but, prior to the arrival of the internal combustion engine, when goods were being moved from place to place, the horsepower calculation was easy – just count the number of horses pulling the cart, or ask the Carter.

Not to be outdone by the canal boatmen and foundry boys, the carters had missions in the city too. Information about them is scarce but there was one on the south side of the city in Spring Lane. Also, there is a report in the Glasgow Herald dated Monday 16th March 1868 about a Mrs Fleming who died accidentally near Great Eastern Road. It records that, at her funeral service, a deputation from Camlachie Carter's Mission took part. It is believed that their venue was in Holywell Street which was taken over by the Brethren and became the George Lyon Memorial Hall.

An amusing anecdote is told about one of the old carters :

A very well-known Christian carter was Jock Brown. He was often in charge of a group of two pairs of powerful Clydesdale horses which were used to haul heavy goods from the foot of West Nile Street, just outside where the old Post Office stood, up the hill to the goods depot of former Buchanan Street railway station (no longer in existence).

The story is told that on one occasion, with the cart fully loaded, the horses stubbornly refused to move. After numerous unsuccessful attempts to get them to proceed, Jock finally transferred one of the horses from the rear pair into the front, and vice versa, and immediately without further difficulty they began to haul the load uphill as required.

> As they moved off, Jock was heard to say of the front horse, "That yin'll no pull unless it's in the lead."

CASTLE STREET MISSION

This mission disappeared in the mega redevelopment which took place in the Townhead area. The leader was a man called James McNab. One memory which was shared regarding this man was that before going on the platform for a Saturday night meeting, the speaker was taken into a side room where Mr McNab took off his jacket, got down on his knees and fervently prayed that the Lord would take control of the meeting. Experiences like this leave an indelible impression on the minds of those present and provide an encouragement to aim higher in the work of the Kingdom.

CLYDE STREET MISSION

The Anderston Free Church of Scotland was built in 1844. Seven years later – in 1851 - the church opened a mission in Anderston to reach out and provide practical assistance to the poor living in the area. The Free Church was one of several which operated its own missions in the city.

The Free Anderston Mission Hall in Clyde Street, c.1880.

DOUGLAS MISSION

This Mission was founded by a Mr Douglas for Christian work among children but evolved into the Douglas Mission with meetings for adults as well as children. The hall was situated in Harvie Street in the city's Ibrox district – well-known because a reasonably famous football team has their stadium there!

The building was erected during the depression years to help those who were suffering through unemployment. A free breakfast for children was served on Sunday mornings.
Two of their workers eventually moved into full-time Christian service. One was Andrew Stewart, who became superintendent of the Seamen's Bethel in Brown Street.
The other was David Orrock, who went into the Church of Scotland ministry and laboured in Lenzie Union Church for many years. On active service during the 1939–1945 World War, he was captured by the Japanese and was among the many who suffered so much during the building of the bridge over the River Kwai.

GRACE STREET MISSION

This outreach was situated in the Finnieston district and was overseen by a father and son duo named Walter and Gavin McAllister.

GROVE STREET INSTITUTE

This was another large building in the north of the city. Grove Street and many of the adjoining streets have now totally disappeared as the elevated section of the M8 motorway cuts through the heart of the area. Robert Logan, who ultimately went to Bethany Hall and then to the Tent Hall, was superintendent there for many years. On moving to Bethany Hall, he was succeeded by George Hood, an Ayrshire man from Mauchline. He was a highly respected Christian leader in the city – always immaculate in his appearance – and with a widespread interest in Evangelistic work throughout the city.

When the hall had to close due to motorway construction, considerable compensation was paid and a very fine suite of halls was built in Ellesmere Street in Hamiltonhill. However, the work itself was never the same. It was a rough area of the city – not safe for people walking up from the nearest public transport and not safe for parking a car; eventually the work had to be abandoned and a closing service was held on 28 February 1993. For some time after this, the premises were used by Prison Fellowship as a drop-in centre.

HIGH STREET MISSION

This work dates back to about 1937 and has been largely dependent on the loyalty of one family.

The original premises were in Duke Street almost opposite the Great Eastern Hotel, a men's lodging house. One man remembers that John Sim, the secretary, had blackboards in every window and updated them every week with details of the future programmes he had arranged. Sadly, John was knocked down and killed while crossing the road but his nephew, David McCaffery and his wife continue his commitment. In later years they moved to other premises further along Duke Street and, later still, to the present building at 269, High Street, one of the last surviving example of the *shop-front* halls.

The picture below shows that, right next door to the Mission, is another feature of bygone days in Glasgow – a *wally close*!

LAMBHILL STREET MISSION

This was a shop front venue set among the tenements in the Kinning Park district and, like many others, has long since disappeared. Two elderly ladies ran this Gospel work – Miss McLean and her sister Mrs McCracken. It was also known as Olivet Hall.

LODGING HOUSE MISSION

This Mission, which was run by the Church of Scotland, was situated in East Campbell Street just off the Gallowgate and east of Glasgow Cross.

It was a large hall and, at meeting times, was populated by row after row of men and women, many of whom were unkempt and shabbily dressed with not a few of them showing visible signs of the alcohol that held them in its bondage. Because of this, they could not give full attention when the programme was in progress and, for very obvious reasons, the *aroma* could be quite overwhelming.

How true Christ's words, *"The thief cometh not, but for to steal, and to kill, and to destroy:"*

MARYHILL MISSION

This was better known as "Mrs Connor's"; Mrs Connor was assisted by her daughter Greta in the work and, like the other missions, it met the need of the times.

MEDICAL MISSION

This Mission lasted for a long number of years and the person in charge during its final years was a Hebrew Christian lady called Cecilia Goldfein.

It was situated in the south side of the city in Oxford Street and finally moved to South Portland Street. Both of these addresses were in the Gorbals district.

It contained a dispensary and medical help was available to all who needed it. Prior to the launch of the National Health Service in 1948, it was a particularly valuable ministry.

PADDY BLACK'S MISSION

This was situated in the Tradeston district on the south bank of the River Clyde. Paddy Black was reputedly a great man and, after his death, the work was carried on by his son James.

Invitations to preach at the Mission were always done in writing and, included with the invitation was a pre-printed reply card. When the booked date was approaching, the reply card was returned to the speaker with the words "To Remind You" overprinted on it.

This gave no excuse for a speaker to forget his promise and also avoided the modern day church secretary syndrome where I have personally known their making double (and once treble!) bookings.

PARTICK BETHEL

This was a good work led by a small man named George Hart. Apparently he lived to be a great age and was referred to as "Methuselah Junior."

After his death, the congregation became affiliated with the Church of the Nazarene and they are still active today in the west of the city.

SCOTSTOUN MISSION

This was situated in Fore Street, a thoroughfare parallel to Dumbarton Road in the Scotstoun neighbourhood. Led for a time by Mr & Mrs Fleming.

SEAMEN'S BETHEL (SEAMEN'S CHAPEL)

This building stood at the corner of Broomielaw and Brown Street. Prior to the construction of the Kingston Bridge, ships used to berth at Broomielaw and the chapel was used for services while amenities were provided for recreational activities. The one time leader of the work, Sandy Galbraith, was a highly respected name in Christian circles. He was followed by Willie Climie and then Andrew Stewart.

Willie Climie

Mr Climie had two assistants – Bob Clapham and John Moore.

Bob Clapham moved on to Arbroath Town Mission where, for over 60 years, he did a sterling work and inaugurated the annual Arbroath Christian Convention.

John Moore moved to become assistant superintendent to James Haxton at the Tent Hall and succeeded Mr Haxton on his sudden death in 1952.

Together with Andrew Stewart and Peter Donald they formed the Superintendents' Trio and sometimes made it a quartet by importing Bob Clapham from Arbroath. All of the four were excellent singers. The picture below shows the four men in singing mode.

The Superintendents' Quartet
Peter Donald, John Moore, Andrew Stewart, Bob Clapham

SEAMEN'S BETHEL

Sometimes referred to as the *South Side Bethel*, this was located in Eaglesham Street. Like the Brown Street Mission, this work was run by the Seamens' Christian Friend Society.

After the closure of the work on 26 May 1976, the Seamens' Chapel continued and then became known as the Seamens' Bethel.

THE TOLBOOTH MISSION

This was situated just east of Glasgow Cross. The leader for many years was Alex Warren, a Glasgow councillor and a J.P. One person's memory of the building was that it was painted in bright pillar box red and therefore not particularly relaxing to the eye! The leaders who followed Alex Warren were Frank Nicholls, John White and Tom Murray; Tom was a very enthusiastic fellow and, while he was there, was greatly supported by his wife Betty and other members of her family. Also, by that time, the red paint had been superimposed with a more suitable shade of cream!

YOKER MISSION

This Mission is situated on Dumbarton Road just west of the old ferry slip and is still active today. It is now known as Yoker Evangelical Church and, in February 2014, they celebrated their Centenary.

The work was originally pioneered in 1913 by two men, Mr James Crawford and Mr James Wood and the historical record of their meeting each other reveals the providential hand of God at work.

Yoker is situated next door to Clydebank and during the second world-war the area was blitzed by the German Luftwaffe. During this operation over 500 people were killed and more than 600 were injured. In spite of this, every effort was made to maintain the church services. The booklet, which was published for the Centenary, records an incident from this time :

> During this conflict God marvellously preserved the hall – a mainly wooden structure – when in March 1941 an incendiary bomb came through the roof, smashed through a door and landed on the floor. It burned its way through the timber, miraculously without starting a general conflagration and burned out harmlessly on the ground beneath.

As the Fellowship developed over the years, new buildings were built and extended. Changes were made to leadership in both personnel and ministry.

In a foreword to their centenary publication, Bill Blair, the senior elder, summarises the reasons for the continued growth in Yoker Evangelical Church.

> How does the work of God progress? It progresses by God's grace through prayer and a loyal, willing and committed membership. It is when we work together as "one body in Christ" that we see Him at work in our Church. As we look back we can only say that we have been truly blessed through the foundation that was laid all these years ago.

Inside the Church with their motto "God First"

Chapter Twelve

THESE ARE THE DAYS

The picture below, taken in the Tent Hall, looks very similar to the one on page 29. However, there is a gap of at least ten years between them; the first one was taken when Mr Haxton was Superintendent, the one below was taken when Mr Troup was the man in charge (see magnified section).

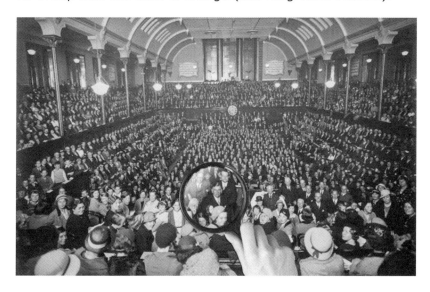

The common denominator between the two photographs is that, in both years, the seats in the venue were covered in people. Every seat full!

Switching attention to the Bethany Hall, the picture below was taken at their Sunday School Trip in Rouken Glen. I have been to many Sunday School events in my lifetime, but I can honestly say that none of them were on the scale shown in the photograph. On the left of the picture, there are some men in uniform; they were Glasgow Corporation tram drivers who transported the *weans* and mothers by *caurs* from London Road in Bridgeton across the River Clyde to the south side of the city. We cannot exactly date the picture but it was in the inter-war period. The reason for showing this scene is to again emphasise the *every seat full* message.

It is when we look at historical scenes like these that we realise how much our national culture has changed over the years. Those *were* the days but they no longer *are* the days! Nostalgia always wears rose-tinted spectacles and this is probably why our selective memory tends to major on the *good* of the *good old days* and play down the *bad* of the *bad old days*. But they both co-existed.

Glasgow has changed and, in many ways, for the better. As we walk around the city centre, we observe that the skyline contains many giant cranes, denoting the fact that new modern buildings are being constructed to house the new state-of-the-art industries that the city is now attracting. No longer is it huge sites to accommodate foundries and shipbuilding yards but purpose-built premises to house the many personnel involved in the hardware, software and

technology required to service the e-world in which we find
ourselves living today.

Technology & Innovation Centre, George Street

The old and the new co-exist in Ingram Street

It's great to experience the buzz in Glasgow now but the city *has* definitely changed. We have more buses, trains, subways, taxis and shops than at any time before but the *every seat full* signs are now stored away in the Church cupboards because they are no longer required.

Society has changed too, not only in Glasgow but also in the country. The reverence for God, which was once a national feature, has slowly dissipated over the decades and we are now living in a totally secular society. Our politicians today have little problem in passing laws which blatantly contravene the principles and high standards laid down by God in His Word and we are paying an increasingly high price for their doing so.

In closing this final chapter, I would like to leave, for your contemplation, the dominant feature which I noted during my many hours of study and consideration of the Mission Halls of Glasgow. That feature was the amount of time allocated to prayer in the weekly schedules of the Missions and the many hours of intercession spent by workers on their knees making them effective.

We would all love to see a return to times of Divine blessing and while we can modernise our methods and presentation of the Gospel message, unless we play our part and cover them in prayer, should we expect God to do His part in the conviction and salvation of souls?

A closing thought from St Mungo, the patron saint of Glasgow, spoken *lang syne* in a sermon. It was his prayer back then and I trust it is our prayer today :

**LET GLASGOW FLOURISH
BY THE PREACHING OF THY WORD
AND THE PRAISING OF THY NAME**

Thanks & References

THANKS

Gordon Haxton

From the beginning of this book project some years ago, I have been helped by many people, as the list below will show but I must particularly thank Gordon Haxton for his continual – or should it be *continuous* – help. To the word *help*, add advice, guidance, correction (facts and grammar!), proof-reading but, above all, encouragement. His knowledge, and recall, of things Glaswegian – both Spiritual and secular, is encyclopaedic.
I could not have done it without him – he is one of God's special saints!

Derick Bingham

I had written a first draft of the first chapter and Derick Bingham, the world-famous Bible Teacher from Northern Ireland was staying in our home over a weekend. I gave him the draft to read and, having done so, he said, "Why don't you entitle the book *Virtue from Adversity?*" I agreed to do this not realising that, when Jean and I dropped him at Aberdeen Airport two days later, we would never see him again this side of Heaven. The following week he was admitted into hospital in Belfast, diagnosed with leukaemia and went to be with his Lord almost a year later.

Others

The list below contains the names of other people who have provided me with input for this book. I hope I have not omitted anyone; if I have, I offer my apologies!
The names are in alphabetical order and, as you will see, some of them have been promoted to Glory since our interviews took place. I cherish their input and involvement.

David Boon	Eva Campbell	Gibbie Campbell
Andrew Carter	Bob Clapham (deceased)	Dudley Clark
Peter Donald	Mary Elliot (deceased)	Syd Elliott
Anna Forrest	Alastair Fraser	Bill Gilvear
Colin Gibb	Jim Givan	Sandy Laird
Andrew Low	Jim McKellar	George McNair
John Moore	Dr George Mitchell	George Murray (deceased)
George Owens	Ian Stangoe	Dr Bill Thompson
Jack Wallace	Ada Ward	James Young

REFERENCES

Title	Date	Author / Publisher	Source

Chapter 1

Photo of Springburn Road			Springburn Library

Chapter 2

Photo of Bridgegate	1904		The Mitchell Library
Report on the Religious Condition of Glasgow	1871	Association for Promoting the Religious and Social Improvement of the City	The Mitchell Library
Minutes of Inaugural Meeting of the Christian Institute – 09/09/1873	1873	The Christian Institute	The Mitchell Library
Lessons for the Time	1879	Rev. A.N. Sommerville DD	The Mitchell Library
Report of Opening of the Christian Institute	1879	North British Daily Mail – 11/10/1879	The Mitchell Library
Photo of the Christian Institute	1911		The Mitchell Library
A Book of Remembrance	1924	G.U.E.A.	Sandy Laird
Minutes of Management Committee of Christian Institute – 11/02/1929	1929	The Christian Institute	The Mitchell Library

Chapter 3

A Book of Remembrance	1924	G.U.E.A.	Sandy Laird
Photo of Saturday Meeting			Gordon Haxton
Festive Season programmes			Sandy Laird

Chapter 4

A Book of Remembrance	1924	G.U.E.A.	Sandy Laird
Photo of Bridgeton Cross			GlescaPals

Chapter 5

Photo of the Institute			The Mitchell Library
The Final Report	1966	Canal Boatmen's Institute	Mary Elliot
Photo of children in Cowcaddens	1910		The Mitchell Library

Chapter 6

A Short History of the Glasgow City Mission		Glasgow City Mission	The Mitchell Library
First Annual Report	1827	Glasgow City Mission	The Mitchell Library
145th Annual Report	1970	Glasgow City Mission	The Mitchell Library
Photo of children in Logan Street Mission			David Boon

Title	Date	Author / Publisher	Source

Chapter 7

Photos of Garngad Choir and Band		Centenary Brochure	Jack Wallace

Chapter 8

One Hundred Years of Church and Mission	2007	Lambhill Evangelical Church	Colin Gibb
Band Testimony	1945	The Band Committee	Jim Givan
Photo of the Band	1945		Colin Gibb

Chapter 9

A Century of Service	1996	Maryhill Evangelical Church	
Jubilee 1887-1937	1937	Springburn Railway Mission	Ada Ward
A Great Little Man	1958	The Sykes Family	
Photo of Springburn Railway Mission			Eva Campbell
Photo of Bill and Betty Smith			Ada Ward
Photo of Springburn By-pass			University of Strathclyde Digital Library

Chapter 10

The Story of the Tabernacle	1899	McNaughtan & Sinclair	Gordon Haxton
Pastor D.J. Findlay	1949	Alexander Gammie	Gordon Haxton
Photo of Male Voice Festival			Gordon Haxton

Chapter 11

The History of Bardowie Street Mission	2007	Sadie Buchanan	Colin Gibb
Yoker Mission Centenary Brochure	2014		Jim McKellar

Chapter 12

Photo of Service in the Tent Hall			I.C.C., Glasgow
Photo of Bethany Hall Sunday School Trip			Mae Haxton